Ken Saro-Wiwa

# OHIO SHORT HISTORIES OF AFRICA

This series of Ohio Short Histories of Africa is meant for those who are looking for a brief but lively introduction to a wide range of topics in African history, politics, and biography, written by some of the leading experts in their fields.

# Ken Saro-Wiwa

## Roy Doron and Toyin Falola

OHIO UNIVERSITY PRESS

ATHENS

Ohio University Press, Athens, Ohio 45701
ohioswallow.com
© 2016 by Ohio University Press
All rights reserved

Printed in the United States of America
Ohio University Press books are printed on acid-free paper ⊗ ™

26 25 24 23 22 21 20 19 18 17 16     5 4 3 2 1

Cover design by Joey Hi-Fi

**Library of Congress Cataloging-in-Publication Data**

Names: Doron, Roy, author. | Falola, Toyin, author.
Title: Ken Saro-Wiwa / Roy Doron and Toyin Falola.
Description: Athens, Ohio : Ohio University Press, 2016. | Series:
  Ohio short histories of Africa | Includes bibliographical references
  and index.
Identifiers: LCCN 2016004173| ISBN 9780821422014 (paperback) |
  ISBN 9780821445501 (pdf)
Subjects: LCSH: Saro-Wiwa, Ken, 1941– | Authors, Nigerian—20th
  century—Biography. | Political activists—Nigeria—Biography. |
  BISAC: BIOGRAPHY & AUTOBIOGRAPHY / General. | SOCIAL
  SCIENCE / Agriculture & Food. | LITERARY COLLECTIONS /
  African.
Classification: LCC PR9387.9.S27 Z64 2016 | DDC 823/.914 [B]—
  dc23
LC record available at https://lccn.loc.gov/2016004173

# Contents

# Illustrations

**Figures**

**Maps**

# Preface

Kenule Saro-Wiwa's execution in 1995 shocked the world and provoked widespread condemnation of the military rule of General Sani Abacha in Nigeria. Though Saro-Wiwa is best known for his activism against the Nigerian state and Shell Oil's destruction of his Ogoni homeland and his defiant stance in the face of his illegal and immoral execution, the man himself was infinitely more complex. This new volume in the Ohio Short Histories of Africa series paints a more complete picture of the man and the many roles he played during his life: human rights and environmental activist, student of the arts, businessman, author, and government official.

This volume showcases a man who transcends African history and who remains, especially since his execution, an icon of human rights and environmental activism. Saro-Wiwa was not only a champion of human rights and a fighter against environmental degradation in his Ogoni homeland; he was also a prolific writer who helped redefine African literature. His voice was not limited to the printed word, however. He wrote extensively for stage and screen, used his artistic fame on Nigerian television to publish children's books, and created one of the most important publishing houses in Nigeria. His fame was his springboard to political action.

Unlike other works on Ken Saro-Wiwa, this book provides the student, scholar, or casual reader a clear and concise introduction to Saro-Wiwa's life, his works, and the importance of his legacy in Nigeria and around the world. The book serves as a guide to the reader interested in Saro-Wiwa's literary career, his environmental and human rights work, and his brushes with the military regime in Nigeria and eventual execution. This book provides an overview of his life as a whole and melds the various aspects of his life into a coherent whole while remaining mindful of the intent of the Short Histories of Africa series.

Though the book follows a chronological approach to Saro-Wiwa's life, several aspects of his biography and achievements overlap, such as his activities in the private sector and his writings. These discussions provide context to his work, life, and career and yet remain accessible to the casual reader.

Saro-Wiwa was a polarizing figure from the beginning of his public life during the Nigerian Civil War, attracting the attention of friends and foes alike. He is also unique in that he left a broad body of literature behind regarding every subject he engaged. As a result, much scholarship regarding his life begins with his words. In addition to his many literary works, novels such as *Sozaboy,* children's books such as the *Basi and*

*Company* series and many others, his various essay collections and memoirs form the backbone of the scholarship on his life, works, and legacy. Though there is no shortage of work on Saro-Wiwa, the closest to a biography of the man comes from his son in the latter's memoir *In the Shadow of a Saint.* This book will serve as a high-profile addition to both the scholarship on Saro-Wiwa and a valuable addition to the Short Histories of Africa series. It provides a unique study of a man whose multifaceted legacy transcends the internal politics of Nigeria and even African Studies. Saro-Wiwa left in his wake a legacy that makes him a truly global figure.

# Introduction

On November 10, 1995, Ken Saro-Wiwa's life ended on a hangman's noose in a prison in Port Harcourt, the victim of one of the Nigerian "Kangaroo Courts" he so enjoyed satirizing. His death, along with eight other activists in the Movement for the Survival of the Ogoni People (MOSOP), catapulted the Ogoni plight to global awareness. The Ogoni Nine, as they became known, were victims of an alleged conspiracy between Shell Oil and the Nigerian military dictatorship headed by General Sani Abacha to silence MOSOP and Saro-Wiwa, one of the most vocal critics of oil exploitation in Nigeria and the environmental costs to the Ogoni people.

Though Saro-Wiwa is best remembered for the activism that cost him his life, he was famous both in Nigeria and abroad for his many achievements. As a respected author, playwright, poet, and television producer, Saro-Wiwa helped redefine the Nigerian novel, creating a body of work that was consciously Nigerian in its conception rather than based on ethnic identity. His memoirs and journalistic work shed light on the ideas he formed as a young man and his political activities during the Nigerian Civil War, when he became military governor of Rivers State and served on the council that helped create the postwar administration. When he felt he could no longer work within an increasingly corrupt and patronage-based system favoring the larger ethnic groups in the country, he left government work and turned to the private sector. Through a series of businesses culminating in the Saros Publishing and Holding companies, he used his private sector wealth to further his goal of creating a Nigerian consciousness that would not be fragmented into Ogoni, Eastern, Christian, or Southern Nigerian cultural manifestations.

Above all, Saro-Wiwa was a nationalist. Throughout his work and personal experience, he learned to love the English language because it made his work accessible to a broad and receptive audience. He regarded English as the unifying language of Nigeria, one of the most ethnic and linguistically diverse countries in the world. He was not an Ogoni nationalist or separatist, but a Nigerian nationalist, albeit a reluctant one. He fought not only to incorporate his people into Nigeria, but to create a Nigeria that would accept all ethnic groups in Nigeria as equal partners in the country.

Although it is possible to examine Saro-Wiwa's life in segments, to do so distorts his legacy. He lived and died dedicated to Nigerian unity and attempted to create a nation out of the fragmented state. All his work in government, entertainment, literature, and activism focused on that goal. In life and death Saro-Wiwa confronted what he saw as the injustice of a Nigerian system that rewarded corruption, nepotism, and regionalism at the expense of merit and minority rights.

Ken Saro-Wiwa was a prolific author who left his mark on the literary world as early as 1973 when his first play, *The Transistor Radio,* was published and produced. His stature as a writer, producer, and journalist gave him a platform to voice his views on Nigerian unity and the place of minorities within the country. His crowning achievement, the hit television series *Basi and Company,* was a landmark work for Nigeria. For the first time, there was a program that was entirely Nigerian, with characters that all Nigerians could recognize and relate to. Though Basi (aka Mr B) occupied a country not of his own creation, Basi made the postcolonial state his own. Similarly, Nigerians needed to coexist in a federation that provided security for all groups, no matter their size and influence. This idea permeated much of Saro-Wiwa's work and gives us a lens by which we can study the life of this unique and sometimes controversial man.

Two closely related events in Nigerian history catapulted Saro-Wiwa to prominence. In 1967, Colonel Chukwuemeka Ojukwu, military governor of the Eastern Region, broke away from Nigeria to form the short-lived Republic of Biafra. Thirty months of intense civil war culminated in the return of Biafra to Nigeria and the creation of a federal republic, albeit one still under military rule. Unlike many in the nascent republic,

Saro-Wiwa became a vocal supporter of Nigerian unity, actively joining the war effort and becoming the civilian administrator of Bonny (in southeastern Nigeria) before going on to join the newly formed Rivers State assembly. Saro-Wiwa's bold step in supporting Nigerian nationalism came from the realization that the interests of the ethnic minorities in general, and the Ogoni in particular, would be better served as part of a federal Nigeria, where no single ethnic group could dominate.

When Shell discovered oil in the Niger Delta in January 1956, the Delta's economic importance forever changed. For the Ogoni, oil was a curse, as the ensuing years brought economic destruction and environmental devastation. For Saro-Wiwa, the destruction of the environment that people depended on, coupled with the siphoning of oil revenues to the larger ethnic groups who controlled the economic patronage system in Nigeria, amounted to genocide. Saro-Wiwa did not believe the fight could be waged within Nigeria alone. After the failure of Biafran secession in 1970, oil became the economic glue that held Nigeria together, and Saro-Wiwa began organizing his people in a nonviolent struggle to regain their economic and political rights and keep their cultural identity, which he felt were imperiled by environmental destruction and the lack of economic opportunity.

It may seem a contradiction that Saro-Wiwa preached for a unified Nigerian society while working to preserve his ethnic group's identity within the structure of the country, but for him, the ideal Nigeria was one where each ethnic group could be culturally independent and still share equally in the political and economic project that was Nigeria. Thus, the worst injustice was that the Ogoni, his people, who numbered less than half a million, were subsidizing Nigeria with the oil pumped out of their land and in the process destroying their environment to such an extent that the Ogoni way of life could not survive. This book charts the tightrope act performed by a man who saw no contradiction in merging his own cultural ideals into a larger and much more diverse country.

The first chapter explores the colonial Nigeria into which Saro-Wiwa was born. This chapter explores the effects that colonial rule and the transition to independence had on the young Saro-Wiwa, the Ogoni, and state-society relations in Nigeria.

The second chapter discusses Saro-Wiwa's childhood and early career at university, where he dedicated himself to the study of the English language and became a lecturer before the civil war cut short his career in education. Saro-Wiwa's university experiences played an especially important part in his intellectual development and political awareness. His experiences as a young minority student in a multiethnic country planted in him the seed of the desire to show Nigerians that the country they inherited from the British could be forged into an inclusive society, rather than one that was based on ethnic loyalties.

Following Biafra's secession in 1967, Saro-Wiwa took a pro-Nigeria approach to the conflict and became the administrator of the newly formed Rivers State. The third chapter explores this tumultuous period in Nigeria's history and Saro-Wiwa's placement firmly on the Nigerian side. His actions set the stage for his future involvement in Nigerian politics and his ideals for Nigerian unity, setting him increasingly in conflict with the Nigerian civilian and military elites.

The fourth chapter looks at Saro-Wiwa's business interests and his writing career. After leaving governmental work, Saro-Wiwa established several real estate, retail, and publishing companies. These businesses served as a base for his writing career, and he published many of his own works through Saros International, his publishing arm. He also used his fame as a writer to create many more business opportunities, culminating in the hit sitcom *Basi and Company* for the Nigerian Television Authority (NTA), to which he added a series of novelizations, including novels for young readers.

The next three chapters look at the issues surrounding Shell Oil's exploitation of the Niger Delta and the complexities of Saro-Wiwa's response to the destruction of the ecosystem that the Ogoni have depended on for their livelihood for millennia. It was this response, which included the creation of MOSOP, Saro-Wiwa's increasing involvement with global human and environmental rights groups, along with his constant criticisms of internal Nigerian politics, that set him on a collision course with the Babangida and Abacha regimes.

The final chapter explains Saro-Wiwa's multiple legacies and attempts to unify the legacies of Saro-Wiwa the poet, author, businessman, scholar, government official, and human rights and environmental activist into a unified legacy of Saro-Wiwa the man. Ken Saro-Wiwa was a complex person who attracted intense admiration from those who supported his work and fierce hatred from those who felt threatened by the brand of nationalism and unity he represented.

# 1

# Nigeria and
# Saro-Wiwa's World to 1960

Kenule Saro-Wiwa's story is intertwined with the story of the country Lord Lugard created in 1914 when he unified Nigeria into one political entity. Saro-Wiwa's relationship with Nigeria defined much of his life, and his attempts to reform it led to his death. In fact, his life, work, and literary career were largely shaped by the same forces that created the colonial state of Nigeria and shaped the legacy that independent Nigeria inherited on October 1, 1960.

The Ogoni, one of the smallest ethnic groups within Nigeria, struggled throughout the colonial period to achieve official recognition and the government protection and funding that came with it. The Ogoni, like many minorities in Nigeria, faced a long history of oppression and domination by the three largest ethnic groups: the Hausa-Fulani in the north, the Yoruba in the southwest, and the Igbo, who dominated the southeast, where the Ogoni lived.[1] Saro-Wiwa viewed his own life as entwined in this struggle and sought to use his position and influence to help achieve an inclusive Nigerian national identity. In many of his works, most notably his Nigerian Civil War memoir *On a Darkling Plain* and his various activist writings in the early 1990s, he is acutely aware of his predecessors and his place within these struggles.

The Ogoni are one of the smallest ethnic and linguistic groups in Nigeria, residing directly east of Port Harcourt along the eastern edge of the Niger Delta, with a population of roughly half a million. They are made up of several subgroups, each with its own identity, history, and distinct dialect. In fact, like most ethnicities in Nigeria, Ogoni identity has historically been fluid, with groups aligning with and dissociating themselves from the Ogoni, according to constantly shifting political considerations within Nigeria. Traditionally a riverine agrarian people, their economic mainstays are aquatic agricultural production, animal husbandry, and fisheries in the Niger Delta. In fact, the Ogoni live in such close relationship to their land that there is no distinction in the Ogoni language between the name for the people and the name for the land,[2] as Saro-Wiwa was fond of pointing out.

Ogoni origins are contested, both with regard to the oral traditions and with regard to linguistic and archaeological evidence. Moreover, the different groups composing the Ogoni have historically acknowledged little mutual identity, despite common linguistic and cultural practices. Some scholars, such as the late linguist Kay Williamson, rely on oral traditions and linguistic analysis to suggest that the Ogoni migrated to their present location from the Kingdom of Ghana over one thousand years ago. Others cite a combination of migration and absorption patterns with local communities as the origin of the Ogoni people. However, their incorporation into the broader Nigerian colonial state forced the Ogoni to organize into a political unity, despite the fact that some Ogoni groups had long rejected the idea of a pan-Ogoni identity.[3]

For Saro-Wiwa, British rule in southern Nigeria, which formally began in 1900 and ended in 1960, ushered in a new phase in interethnic relations. British rule concentrated power over the country and its resources along ethnic lines; it created a system that encouraged resource exploitation, and ethnicity became the de facto mode for political organization. This system, which the British called "indirect rule," gave rise to a struggle for access to the mechanisms determining political culture after independence. Saro-Wiwa decried this system, not only because it shaped the ethnically fractured structure of postcolonial Nigeria, but more importantly, because it gave rise to a system of exploitation that he called "indigenous imperialism."

Although the British did not invent ethnic and political conflict in Nigeria, they created a system in which the only legitimate access to resources and the mechanisms of distribution was organized along ethnic lines. In his civil war memoir Saro-Wiwa lambasted the Igbo for denouncing this system for marginalizing them at the national level but failing to acknowledge that the same system allowed them to dominate political institutions in the southeast of the country at the expense of the smaller groups whom they shut out of government appointments and contracts.

From the establishment of colonial rule in Nigeria at the end of the nineteenth century until 1914, the British created several protectorates, which eventually coalesced into the Protectorate of Northern Nigeria and the Colony and the Protectorate of Southern Nigeria. As with most colonial possessions, the British administered the protectorates through a system of local rulers, known collectively as "indirect rule," as mentioned earlier. In the Northern Nigeria Protectorate, the British relied heavily on established local rulers, usually emirs remaining from precolonial times, to administer the protectorate and collect taxes. In the much more politically diverse Southern Protectorate, many differing local administrations emerged, owing to British recognition of the multiplicity of precolonial political systems. The British colonial administration co-opted those systems as important mechanisms in colonial administration. However, some aspects of precolonial rule, especially revenue collection systems, were incompatible with the new system of government.

A major change that the British enacted in both Northern and Southern Nigeria was to shift the tax collection system to one that required payment in coin and paper, namely, the British pound. This change required a retooling of local economies that had for centuries accepted payment either in specie or in commodities. The Protectorate of Southern Nigeria was better suited to this new system because many parts of the region had well-established import/export economies that replaced the slave trade in the early nineteenth century. Further, alcohol sale in the south provided a ready tax base and served as one of the major revenue generators for the colonial administration in Southern Nigeria, whereas strict religious laws in the predominantly Muslim north forbade the sale and consumption of alcohol. As a result, Northern Nigeria hemorrhaged money because the tax collection system did not generate the necessary revenues to finance the colonial government. By 1912, Northern Nigeria was heavily dependent on subsidies, both from the southern protectorate and an annual allocation of GBP 300,000 from the Colonial Office.

Sir Frederick Lugard (later Lord), who previously served as high commissioner of Northern Nigeria, was recalled to the country from his post as the governor of Hong Kong in 1912 to facilitate the unification of Northern and Southern Nigeria into one administrative unit. The main goals of Nigerian unification were economic in nature. First and foremost, Lugard needed to stabilize the finances of the Northern Protectorate and allow for easier transfer of funds between the different regions of the country. Second, Lugard was to create a unified bureaucracy to make administering Nigeria more cost-effective and efficient.

Lugard articulated British policy toward Nigeria in a book called *The Dual Mandate in British Tropical Africa.* In it, he outlined the idea of indirect rule and the creation of native institutions. Lugard envisioned a system whereby the colonial administration would serve British interests while working in the best interests of the colonized people. In particular, Lugard encouraged local control over taxation and expenditures and discouraged British officials from interfering in local affairs. In Northern Nigeria, where Lugard had previously served as high commissioner, he maintained most of the tax collection system prevalent before British rule. The emir collected the taxes, paid his officials, and financed other projects from a "native treasury" created for this purpose. This system worked because of a long history of centralized rule and taxation in the precolonial states, especially the powerful Sokoto Caliphate. In the south, there was little history of direct taxation. State revenue extraction took the form of customs duties, court fees and fines, and other administrative fees and duties, such as the aforementioned tax on alcohol sales. These policies made revenue allocation in the south a colonial creation, whereas in the north, the colonial administration superimposed itself on an existing taxation system. Finally, Lugard separated colonial administration from the "native treasuries" and required that all local administrative salaries come exclusively from local revenue collection; they could not be supplemented by outside funds.

Despite pretensions of allowing native rulers to administer their own populations, local rulers were little more than unofficial colonial agents, lacking autonomy and political clout. Further, Lugard homogenized the multiple administrative systems in the south, which he dismissed as chaotic and wasteful, but the reorganizaton resulted in increased marginalization of smaller ethnic groups. Most damaging, Lugard created a new type of indigenous ruler in the southern region modeled on the northern emir. This departure from the existing heterogeneity in southern Nigeria created a new class of rulers and bestowed on them powers that few rulers in the south had traditionally possessed. In effect, Lugard created a new class of native colonial administrators who owed their allegiance to their respective ethnic groups but derived their power, not from traditional roles, but from new roles acquired from the British administration. The three major ethnic groups, namely, the Hausa-Fulani in the north, the Yoruba in the southwest, and the Igbo in the southeast, used the new colonial administration to consolidate their power and create a new colonial patronage system that benefited their own groups at the expense of the many minority ethnic groups in the country, including Saro-Wiwa's Ogoni.

Despite the lack of shared identity as Ogoni before British colonial occupation, British administrators recognized the various Ogoni groups as a distinct "tribe." In 1932, most Ogoni-speaking areas were amalgamated into what the British determined as the Ogoni "tribe," with various subgroups referred to as "clans." In reality, no stable affiliations of this kind existed; for example, one group related to the Ogoni, the Eleme, petitioned the British to be included as part of the Ogoni, but in later years dissociated themselves from the Ogoni. This ethnic and linguistic grouping of peoples into political units was not unique to the Ogoni, however, and in the aftermath of unification, many smaller ethnic groups realized that strength in numbers was the only way to secure their collective rights. Other new ethnopolitical groups coalesced, especially in the diverse Niger Delta region, with the Ijo and the Andoni securing similar recognition from the British authorities. Larger groups in Nigeria were not immune to this consolidation of political power along similar lines. Under British rule, the Yoruba in the southwest of Nigeria transformed from a patchwork of opposing kingdoms and city-states into a major unified force in Nigerian politics, both during colonial rule and after. Similarly, the Igbo, largely recognized as a stateless society, merged into a political force that attempted to secede from Nigeria and form the Republic of Biafra in 1967, sparking a three-year civil war.

For the Ogoni, the need for political influence became increasingly important. In 1945, as various ethnic groups merged and new ethnic identifications surfaced, the Ogoni created the Ogoni Central Union (OCU). Led by Paul Birabi, the first Ogoni university graduate, the OCU agitated for an official Ogoni administrative division. After attaining this in 1947 with the creation of an

Ogoni division within what was at the time the Rivers Province, Birabi and the OCU fought for increased access to colonial funds.

The 1950s proved especially troublesome for the Ogoni. As British rule neared its end, the colonial government ceded more and more authority to the native administrations, dominated by Yoruba, Igbo, and Hausa elites. In 1954, the British codified the three major ethnic divisions by splitting the country into three regions, each dominated by one of the major ethnic groups. Birabi pushed for increased Ogoni participation in the new Eastern Region, which, though dominated by the Igbo, was also the most ethnically diverse and densely populated of the three regions. The OCU succeeded in obtaining some funding, especially for access to government-sponsored education for Ogoni youth. Saro-Wiwa, who enrolled at the Government College Umuahia in 1954 at age thirteen, was one of the early beneficiaries of this program.

In the mid- to late 1950s, as Nigeria edged closer to independence, political rivalries born under the colonial administration intensified. The three largest political groups, the Hausa-Fulani, Yoruba, and Igbo, were set to dominate the political arena in the emerging state. This reality, codified by the regional boundaries the British imposed in 1954, led to increased protests among the smaller groups in the country, including the Ogoni. In an attempt to allay minority fears, the British convened a commission headed by Sir Henry Willink in

1957, intending to create safeguards ensuring minority rights in independent Nigeria. Many of the minorities, such as the Ijo, Ibibio, and, most prominently, the minorities in the Western Region agitated for political separation from the "big three" groups as the only way to safeguard their rights from regional ethnic domination. The commission ultimately decided that "although there remained a Body of genuine fears and the future was regarded with real apprehension . . . a separate state would not provide a remedy for the fears expressed."[4] Rather, the commission suggested that the major issues facing the minorities would be better served by handling their concerns at the federal level.

The commission determined that regionalism in Nigeria would do little but destabilize the country and that constitutional safeguards specifically protecting minority rights at the national level would be the best guarantee of these liberties. Thus, despite the protestations of many minority groups testifying before the commission and who saw that a federal solution would be the best guarantor of minority rights, the commission found that these rights would best be secured by a system created for, and dominated by, the three major groups.

Minority fears of domination echoed Saro-Wiwa's own fears. In fact, during the Nigerian Civil War he actively supported the Nigerian state, stating that "the true interest of [the ethnic minorities in Nigeria] lay in a more equitable country where all groups would be fairly treated, where all groups had self-determination. Biafra was not that country."[5] However, his views echoed those expressed in the Minorities Commission Report, especially regarding Ogoni domination by the larger ethnic political groups in the country. For him, as it was for many in Nigeria, this was not merely domination, but a form of imperialism, virtually indistinguishable from the British variety in its domination and oppression of minority rights.

The 1950s also saw one of the most important developments for the future of Nigeria: the discovery of rich petroleum deposits in the Niger Delta. This discovery proved disastrous for the Ogoni. In 1956, Shell-BP discovered oil in the town of Oloibiri, in the southern Niger Delta near the town of Brass. In 1958, the first commercial drilling began. This quickly transformed the Niger Delta and the Nigerian economy as a whole. The oil revenue came under the control of the ruling elites. As government revenues came to depend almost exclusively on the petroleum sector, the Niger Delta, including Ogoni lands, became the main source of government funds, effectively subsidizing the Nigerian government and, unofficially, its corrupt officials before and especially after independence. Though oil exploitation and the destruction of the Ogoni environment are discussed in a separate chapter, the colonial government system that continued into independence ensured that the Ogoni, and most of the other ethnicities in Nigeria, saw their lands and the profits from those lands redistributed among the powerful elites that controlled the country.

When Lord Lugard orchestrated Nigeria's unification in 1912–14, he sought to create a more efficient, economically unified political entity. Lugard began a process, continued by subsequent British administrators, which transformed the Nigerian economy and the relations among its various societies. When Nigeria became independent on October 1, 1960, tensions within the country intensified as competing groups already vying for a stake in the British colonial system fought for control and influence over a diverse, resource-rich state struggling to transform itself into a self-sufficient nation.

In the early years of Nigerian independence, the country lurched from crisis to crisis as the pains of a political system built on ethnic sectionalism and

Map 1.1 Nigeria to 1967

mistrust overshadowed the euphoria of liberation from British colonial rule. Almost immediately after independence, the drive for the federalization of the country was renewed, culminating in 1963 with the creation of the Midwestern Region.

The creation of the new region did little to alleviate ethnic or religious tension in the country. In 1962, the Nigerian government undertook a census to determine, among other things, parliamentary seat allocation in anticipation of the 1963 general election. In the previous elections, held in 1959, the Northern People's Congress (NPC) won 134 of the 314 seats in the House of Representatives, despite winning only 28.2 percent of the vote. The predominantly southern coalition, National Council of Nigeria and the Cameroons (NCNC), won 36.1 percent of the vote, but because of parliamentary allocation, secured only 89 seats. A predominantly western coalition, the Action Group (AG), won 27.6 percent of the vote but secured only 73 seats due to the same electoral system. This political system, which so heavily favored the Northern Region, meant that southerners found the temptation irresistible to remedy this inequity with creative census procedures.[6] Initial census figures released in May 1963 showed that the Western and Eastern regions' populations increased by 70 percent in the decade since the 1953 census. The Northern Region's population grew by only 30 percent in the same period. As a result, the NPC government ordered a second census to be taken, where the population numbers in the north were adjusted to meet the reported growth in the south, thus maintaining the status quo in parliament.

Both the 1964 general election and the 1965 Western Region election were as corrupt as the census. In order to wrest control from the NPC, the AG and NCNC united with smaller parties from the north to form a new coalition called the United Progressive Grand Alliance (UPGA). Some in the southern parties, led by the unpopular Western Region premier, Samuel Akintola, feared a UPGA victory. Akintola formed a new southern party called the Nigerian National Democratic Party (NNDP) and united with the NPC to form the Nigerian National Alliance (NNA). UPGA activists were arrested en masse in the north; in one case in Kano 297 UPGA campaigners were detained, with some held until after the elections and others released and ordered to return to their homes in the south. UPGA candidates were denied access to the ballots, resulting in 50.57 percent of the Northern Region seats going unopposed to NNA candidates. As a result of these tactics, the NCNC boycotted the elections and only agreed to contest them on March 18, 1965, after NCNC leader Nnamdi Azikiwe secured concessions from the NPC head and the prime minister, Abubakar Tafawa Balewa.

These tactics eroded Nigerians' faith in the electoral system. The next election, in the Western Region, further reinforced this distrust. Akintola's NNDP vowed to win the election by any means necessary. According to Saro-Wiwa, "NNDP politicians threatened to win, whether the electorate voted or not. And win they did! In some cases, the results were declared before the ballot boxes were opened!"[7] The NNDP engaged in massive electoral rigging, and infighting among the AG and NCNC resulted in candidates from these parties running against each other, splitting the vote and ensuring NNDP victories. When results were announced, both sides declared victory, resulting in widespread violence that amounted to a veritable civil war within the Western Region.

Like most in Nigeria's early years of independence, Saro-Wiwa grew to detest the political structure revolving around the large ethnic groups and centering on a north-south divide. This divide naturally focused on the large ethnic groups and the power dynamics between them, while minorities like Saro-Wiwa's Ogoni were excluded.

It was into this political, social, and cultural maelstrom that Kenule Saro-Wiwa was born on October 10, 1941.

## 2

# Saro-Wiwa's Childhood and Education

Ken Saro-Wiwa was born Kenule Beeson Tsaro-Wiwa on October 10, 1941, to Jim Beeson Tsaro-Wiwa and his third wife, Widu, in their home in Bane, the center of the Khana kingdom. Tsaro, or Saro, is the Ogoni honorific for a firstborn son of the family. Kenule went by Tsaro-Wiwa until after the Nigerian Civil War in 1970, during which his government correspondence still used Tsaro-Wiwa. He changed his last name to Saro-Wiwa sometime in the early 1970s, apparently for esthetic purposes.

Saro-Wiwa's father, a forest ranger and business-man, had tried for many years to have children, but his first wife could not bear children, and his second wife suffered a string of miscarriages. Saro-Wiwa's mother had also miscarried several times before Kenule was born. Unsurprisingly, his birth was not a simple one, and he was left for dead five times perhaps due to a congenital heart disorder, but he managed to rally each time. Despite the circumstances of his birth, he was a well-adjusted child. He walked at seven months and re-mained an only child until the age of seven. He was the pride of his family, which later included a sister, Barine, and a brother, Owens.

Saro-Wiwa's early life followed much the same trajectory as that of many children living during the transition in Nigeria from traditional education to the British colonial system. The Ogoni, like many other societies in the Niger Delta, relied heavily on agriculture and aquaculture. Because of this, the traditional education system in Ogoni focused on educating the youth for a life of subsistence farming. One of the primary ways Ogoni youth claimed their place in adult society was through the *Yaa* tradition. Yaa was a ritualistic passage to adulthood in Ogoni society, focusing on the militaristic aspects of defending Ogoni territory along with cultivating respect for the economic and cultural mainstays defining Ogoni culture. This coming-of-age ritual was of paramount importance in traditional Ogoni society but was being supplanted by colonial education. Saro-Wiwa therefore had a hybrid early education: he was enrolled at the Native Authority School in Bori while participating in the traditional educational activities of the Yaa tradition. Despite his weak heart, he excelled at many of these exercises, especially palm wine tapping and various athletic practices. However, by the time Saro-Wiwa was an older child, the Yaa tradition was in decline, being supplanted by formal schooling, and it is not clear whether he completed the formal rituals before he was sent to Government College Umuahia (GCU) in 1954 at the age of fourteen. One of his childhood

36

contemporaries, the Ogoni historian Sonpie Kpone-Tonwe, completed the rite in the early 1950s, stating that the tradition went into steep decline shortly after, with the next performance not held until the mid-1960s, and the last known enactment in 1983. In 1991, he spoke to Saro-Wiwa about documenting the practice with an eye to reviving it and incorporating it into Ogoni education. However, the latter's judicial murder in 1995 ended these plans.[1]

Like many Nigerian institutions, the education system was a blend of local tradition and foreign impositions. Western education in Nigeria had its origins in the Church Missionary Society (CMS) and in the mid-nineteenth-century Catholic schools. Officials of both CMS and the Catholic Church struggled to maintain support for the schools despite the colonial government's promotion of industrial and practical education. The missionary groups were not interested in "practical" education and preferred to focus on religious training. The great Nigerian historian Ade Ajayi pointed out, "They [the CMS and the Catholic Church] sent missionaries to preach the gospel and they promoted education largely because they wished to train teachers and clergymen."[2] Thus, Western education did not necessarily address the social needs of early Nigerian society and was seen mostly as a status symbol for the Nigerian elites in the colonial system.

It was not until the late nineteenth and early twentieth centuries, after Nigeria had been incorporated into the British Empire, that colonial administrators began to address the need for more practical education that would both provide clerks for the colonial bureaucracy and support a class of skilled artisans. The church schools were extremely deficient in this type of training, leading the British government to invest in its own schools. The first was King's College in Lagos, which became one of the most prestigious schools in Nigeria.

The educational shift accelerated in the 1920s; in 1926, the colonial government passed the Education Ordinance, which, among other projects, funded the creation of Government College Umuahia, where Saro-Wiwa began his secondary school education. Before that, Saro-Wiwa was educated in his native Ogoni schools, in his native Khana language. Only a lucky few among Nigerian youths could hope to attend the new secondary schools. Most could only aspire to a basic education, a privation Saro-Wiwa came to see as one of the great impediments to Nigeria's success. In fact, he mocked many aspects of Nigerian education in his many works of fiction, as discussed in chapter 4.

Saro-Wiwa left home to attend GCU in 1954. Though he was the only Ogoni in a school dominated by the Igbo, he always claimed that he felt at home there, because school policy mandated that English was the only language spoken there. Though he was the son of an Ogoni chief, he was admitted to the school on his own merits, excelling in the entrance exam and receiving the prestigious school scholarship for 1954. By the time he graduated in 1961, he had amassed a collection of academic and athletic honors, including prizes for history and English; he was captain of the table tennis team and a starting member of the cricket team.

It was the English language that made him feel Nigerian, and not just Ogoni. In later years, he claimed it was this experience at Umuahia that gave him the hope that Nigeria could rise above its ethnic primacy and create a culture that was truly Nigerian. He embraced English as a way to communicate to the widest possible audience, both in Nigeria and abroad. Although he needed little incentive to excel in his studies, sports, and other activities, a common language fostered an environment where he could find equal footing with the other students, and the school's Latin motto, *In Unum Luceant* (May We Shine as One), became more than just a slogan for the young scholar. English became an important tool that Saro-Wiwa later wielded in his attempts to show all Nigerians that there existed a quintessentially Nigerian culture that could be more inclusive than blood kinship or ethnicity.

As discussed in chapter 1, Nigeria's ethnic and linguistic diversity made the country difficult to govern and reinforced the centrality of ethnicity in the mechanisms of the state. However, at GCU, Saro-Wiwa realized that the English language could unite the disparate ethnic groups and create a sense of community beyond the ethnic rivalries. This belief would follow him throughout most of his life, especially in his most popular work, *Basi and Company,* discussed in chapter 4.

In 1962, Saro-Wiwa left GCU and enrolled at the University of Ibadan (UI); this was the same year the UI severed its association with the University of London and became an independent institution. At UI, Saro-Wiwa continued his academic excellence and cultural contributions. He won the English Department Prize in 1963 and 1965 and a university scholarship in 1963. He was a member of the UI cricket team, as well as president of the school's dramatic society in the 1964–65 academic year. He was also editor of two school newspapers, first *The Mellanbite,* Mellanby Hall's newsletter in 1963–64, and then the university newspaper *The Horizon* the following year. During 1964–65 he also served as chairman of Mellanby Hall. Saro-Wiwa had a much harder time breaking into student government at UI than he did with academics. In contrast to GCU, UI presented a microcosm experience of the deep ethnic divide in Nigeria. There was only one other Ogoni student in the school and none on the faculty or staff. As a result, Saro-Wiwa was considered one of the Igbo, as all Easterners were called. Naturally, the school's student government was dominated by the Yoruba, who constituted the overwhelming majority of the student body. Recalling one election he contested where he felt he was "cheated" on tribal grounds, he lamented, "I once contested a student's Union election and crashed out, winning a majority of votes only in the ladies' hall. That year, the entire elected Executive was solidly Yoruba. I believed that the Yoruba students were so ashamed of this that the following year they did not contest any post at all, enabling a minority student to win."[3]

Another peculiarity that shaped Saro-Wiwa's early life was that he was unusually short. Standing only five foot one, he constantly sought to prove himself, being fond of the expression "What's height got to do with it?" This fact gave rise in the popular imagination to the idea that he suffered from a "Napoleon complex," that he had to overcompensate for his height by demanding attention in other ways. Saro-Wiwa won many university accolades at the University of Ibadan, just as he did at Government College Umuahia. However, it was his love of drama that would dominate his life at university and his later career as a film producer and activist. In 1964, he played Henry IV in a UI production of Shakespeare's play. The university also had a traveling troupe called Theatre-on-Wheels, with which Saro-Wiwa reprised his role in performances in Lagos, Ilorin, Kaduna, Kano, Benin, and Enugu, among other cities across Nigeria. Theatre-on-Wheels received much acclaim, both at home and abroad, collaborating with the prestigious Nottingham Playhouse when they sent a troupe to Nigeria in 1963 featuring the young Dame Judi Dench.

Despite his successes in the theater, he had harbored political ambitions from a young age. The loss of the student union leadership office showed him that Nigeria was entrenched in ethnic rivalry that was unlikely to just disappear on its own. Even before his time at the University of Ibadan, he had taught at Government

College Umuahia, and at Stella Maris College in Port Harcourt and believed that education was the key to resolving cultural conflict. Therefore, he dedicated himself to teaching at UI, and later at the University of Nigeria–Nsukka, in order to help combat these rivalries. Despite this intention, the Nigerian Civil War of 1967 cut short his ambitions of academic life. When the war broke out, he was teaching at the University of Nigeria–Nsukka, which was quickly renamed the University of Biafra. This put him in personal peril due to his support for Nigeria in the conflict; obviously he was unable to continue working at a university in the center of the Biafran nationalist movement.

# The Nigerian Civil War Years

Ken Saro-Wiwa seemed destined for a quiet academic life. However, the chain of events that began with the January 1966 coup forever altered the studious young man's life. When the Nigerian military government, then headed by Major General Yakubu Gowon, transformed the country into a federal republic consisting of twelve states, Saro-Wiwa saw an opportunity to correct the disproportionate power the major ethnic group held in the country and better integrate the Ogoni. He claimed an influential role in this process.

In his memoirs, Saro-Wiwa portrayed himself as a loyal Nigerian citizen trapped inside the secessionist Biafran state. According to Gowon's federal plan, Ogoniland was to be situated within one of the new states carved out of the secessionist Eastern Region, namely Rivers State. Saro-Wiwa managed to position himself as a leader of the Ogoni community within the new Rivers State. After fleeing Biafra, he returned with the conquering Nigerian military and established himself as civilian administrator of the oil depot city of Bonny. His actions established him as an Ogoni leader firmly devoted to Nigeria who would agitate for his people's inclusion in the life of the nation. His new position as a leader was made challenging because of some significant events occurring just before the end of colonial rule, however.

On January 10, 1966, the first meeting of the British Commonwealth prime ministers held outside the United Kingdom convened in Lagos. Sir Abubakar Tafawa Balewa, Nigeria's prime minister, convened the special meeting to discuss steps to end white minority rule in Rhodesia. The gathering showcased Nigeria's growing influence in international affairs and the country's emergence as an important regional power in Africa. However, as the last delegations left the country on the night of January 15, a group of mostly Igbo military officers, known collectively as the Five Majors, attempted to overthrow the Nigerian First Republic and take control of the government in a coup d'état.[1]

General Johnson Aguiyi-Ironsi, the Nigerian chief of staff and also Igbo, quickly quashed the coup the following day. However, Tafawa Balewa died in the attack, along with Ahmadu Bello, the premier of the Northern Region, and his Western Region counterpart Samuel Akintola. Festus Okotie-Eboh, the finance minister, and most of the military's top commanders also died in the bloody attempt. Nnamdi Azikiwe, known popularly as Zik, Nigeria's first president, was in Britain receiving medical treatment and therefore escaped injury.

With the bulk of the First Republic's leadership now dead, the republic itself soon died as well, to be replaced by a series of military dictatorships. Saro-Wiwa was then in his last year at the University of Ibadan. Like many in the country, the events of that night took him by surprise. He later recalled the moment he arrived at the university campus in the early afternoon of January 16 and first learned about the coup: "A coup? Impossible! I did not believe it." By late afternoon, Radio Nigeria confirmed the news, urging calm. However, rather than panic, the campus at the University of Ibadan erupted in celebration: "There was such wild joy, general dance and great jubilation as I had not seen there in all four sessions I had spent in Ibadan. . . . Students forgot themselves in their joy; they embraced and hugged one another, male and female alike."[2]

The scenes Saro-Wiwa described were hardly unique. By 1966, the First Republic had become so unpopular that the coup was initially welcomed across the country, and the jubilant scenes repeated even in Ibadan despite the fact that the Western Region's premier, Akintola, was a victim of the coup attempt. Akintola was not well liked, owing in no small part to the manner in which he ascended to power in the Western Region; he had displaced the visionary Yoruba leader Obafemi Awolowo in 1962 after Akintola orchestrated a riot inside the Western Region's House of Deputies that gave Abubakar's federal government justification to declare a state of emergency in the Western Region and order Awolowo imprisoned. The Yoruba leadership found this so repulsive they refused to cooperate with

Akintola, who was now regarded as a stooge for the Northern-led Northern People's Congress (NPC) federal government. Saro-Wiwa recalled the crisis as showing that "bare-faced opportunism had become the prevailing characteristic of Nigerian politics."[3]

In his memoir, *On a Darkling Plain,* Saro-Wiwa posited a theory of the unfolding of the January coup and why it was remembered as an ethnic Igbo coup. For Saro-Wiwa, the coup was not perpetrated as an Igbo ethnic putsch: "Since 1966, there have been enough coups to convince everyone that a coup is a conspiracy, a dangerous conspiracy, and only friends and trusted associates engage in it." Most of the conspirators were either schoolmates at the various government colleges or otherwise trusted friends belonging to the same military cohort. The fact that many of them were Igbo was the product of British colonial policies that favored Igbo access to school and military institutions and not an explicit attempt to form an exclusively Igbo conspiracy.

This argument did not persuade other Nigerians, especially in the north, who saw the coup as a southern plot to take over the country. Saro-Wiwa detested the political definition of a north-south divide in Nigeria, calling it a dangerous fiction that fed the "cankerworm of tribalism" around the country and oversimplified existing ethnic and linguistic complexities. For Saro-Wiwa, the northerners victimized by the coup consisted of over two hundred unique ethnic, language, and religious groups, and could not be thought of as a single entity. The south was equally heterogeneous, but the Igbo and Yoruba together dominated the political sphere in the south of the country at the expense of the Ogoni, Mbembe, Ijo, and others. Saro-Wiwa concluded that it was "on the basis of such false assumptions, hard lines are taken and hatred bred!"[4]

Ironsi became head of state of the new Federal Military Government (FMG) after the senate president, Nwafor Orizu, handed power to the military, officially ending the Nigerian First Republic. The fact that Orizu, who was Igbo, and President Azikiwe did nothing to attempt a continuation of civilian rule in the wake of the failed coup helped reinforce notions of a broad Igbo conspiracy. To make matters worse, the coup plotters themselves faced no punishment for their mutiny, despite their arrest and the fact that their actions constituted a capital offense. Saro-Wiwa sympathized with Ironsi, reasoning that if the new leader executed the plotters, many in the country who saw the majors as heroes would rebel against him. If he released them, those aggrieved by the coup would act in much the same way. Ironsi's solution was to keep them incarcerated without charge, a ploy he hoped would placate both sides, but in reality it only increased rumors of conspiracy. Saro-Wiwa saw Ironsi as a man in an impossible situation, rather than as an active manipulator of the ethnic tensions engulfing the country. Ironsi's regime began on shaky footing and would end after barely six months, when he was assassinated in another coup attempt.

Saro-Wiwa lamented, "We must shed a tear for Ironsi, for he was an honest man."[5]

Saro-Wiwa learned of the second coup as part of a joke when one of his schoolmates approached him and declared, "You are the new premier!" Unlike the celebrations that accompanied the January coup, the atmosphere on the campus at Ibadan in July was tense and insecure. Ironsi, who began his tenure as head of state in an unstable situation, had only exacerbated matters in his attempts to stabilize the country. On May 24, 1966, Ironsi issued Decree No. 34, which abolished the regional federal system of Nigeria, replacing it with a single unitary structure. This move stripped the regional leaders of their power, grouping the various areas of the country into provinces. Additionally, all appointments to the civil service bureaucracy and the military would now be handled by the central government in Lagos.

The reaction to this decree was immediate. Riots erupted across the Northern Region, targeting Igbo and other easterners, whom northerners referred to as *yameri*. Some in the north maintained that the riots that began in May were spontaneous and sparked by Igbo hubris, as they were seen to gloat about their takeover of Nigeria. One apocryphal story placed the blame on an Igbo baker in the city of Kaduna, who adorned his bread with the famous painting of St. George slaying the dragon. In this baker's version, St. George's face was replaced with an image of one of the coup leaders, Chukwuma Kaduna

Nzeogwu, while the dragon represented Ahmadu Bello. However, these riots were far from spontaneous. Saro-Wiwa wrote, "This did not look like a spontaneous affair. It was definitely carefully calculated and was dastardly." Recent historical work, such as Douglas Anthony's, confirm that the riots were planned.[6]

In an effort to stabilize the country, Ironsi organized a national convention in Ibadan to be held on July 30, 1966. The night before, after a party organized at the home of the military governor of the Western Region, Lieutenant Colonel Adekunle Fajuyi, Ironsi and Fajuyi were both abducted and killed, though confirmation of their deaths would be withheld for six months. In the aftermath of the coup, Ironsi's chief of staff, Colonel Yakubu Gowon, was appointed as the new head of state. The coup only intensified the violence against the Igbo in the north. Between August and September, the Igbo suffered further massacres in northern Nigeria; with estimates ranging from 50,000 to 100,000 killed. Ojukwu, still governor of the Eastern Region, called on Igbo living in other parts of Nigeria to return to the east.[7] Igbo from all over the country answered his call. Up to two million people fled to the Igbo heartland, and Ojukwu began to prepare for secession claiming that easterners could no longer live in peace in Nigeria.

Saro-Wiwa, perhaps concerned for his personal safety, boarded a transport to Port Harcourt. He defended the flight of the easterners living in the north, stating that "no responsible leader would have encouraged any

Eastern Nigerian to remain in Northern Nigeria." However, he mocked those from Lagos and Ibadan, calling them weak-minded people who "only needed a word of encouragement and they were instantly on the move back home." It is unclear if he considered himself one of those weak-minded individuals for fleeing Ibadan. On his way to Port Harcourt, he observed the throngs of internally displaced refugees, "the great rush by, particularly, women and children who were being encouraged to return home by their husbands and fathers. It was a sorry sight to see women, their lifelong belongings packed up in shabby bundles, children tied to their backs, fighting their way into the . . . huge lorries travelling to the Eastern Region."[8]

As it became clear that Nigeria was heading toward another crisis, Ghanaian head of state Joseph Ankrah sponsored an attempt at reconciliation between Nigerian factions. In January 1967, eastern and federal leaders met at the resort town of Aburi, near Accra. Though the meetings ended with an agreement, both sides later ignored the provisions in the Aburi Accords, especially the requirement that any decision affecting the entire country be agreed upon by all the military governors. In March, Ojukwu subordinated all federal government offices in the east, including the police and tax collection agencies, to the Eastern Region. This move made the Eastern Region a de facto autonomous region within Nigeria, prompting Colonel Gowon to impose a naval blockade.

By April, Nigeria was on the brink. The FMG had successfully isolated the Eastern Region from the rest of the country and the world by closing the international airports in Port Harcourt and Calabar and suspending all postal service to the east, including money transfers, thereby freezing government employee salaries. Ojukwu, for his part, began smuggling arms into the region and equipping vigilante forces, which he called the Civil Defence, which Saro-Wiwa mockingly referred to as "Simple Defence." These ill-trained soldiers used their newfound power to attack federal police officers and non-Igbo civilians. Ntieyong U. Akpan, head of the civil service in the east throughout the Nigerian Civil War, cited the behavior of these Civil Defence personnel

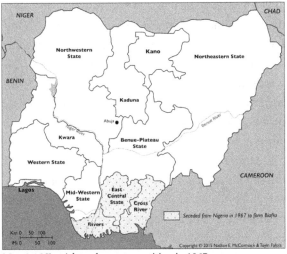

**Map 3.1** Nigeria's twelve-state partition in 1967

as one of the main reasons the smaller ethnic groups quickly became alienated from Biafra.

In May, Gowon attempted some conciliatory steps toward Ojukwu, such as lifting the blockade. After those were met with contempt, Gowon issued Decree No. 8 on May 27, 1967, creating twelve states out of the four regions. Gowon aimed to create a more manageable government and end regional strife by creating smaller political entities that would wield significantly less power than the large regions. The decree had the added effect of further weakening support for the Igbo-dominated regional government in the east. The newly created Rivers State and Cross River State would free the smaller ethnic groups from the Igbo, most of whom would remain in a landlocked East Central State. Ojukwu pounced on the decree as a casus belli and three days later announced his secession from Nigeria, transforming the Eastern Region into the Republic of Biafra.

Eastern Nigeria, though dominated by the Igbo, was the most populous and heterogeneous region in the country. The smaller ethnic groups sat atop most of the major oil deposits, making their land immensely important for both Nigeria's and Biafra's export economies. The federal and Biafran sides both needed to secure the support of the ethnic groups in the region. Some, like Philip Efiong, an Ibibio who became Biafra's chief of staff and Ojukwu's second in command, and Victor Banjo, a Yoruba colonel, sided immediately with Biafra. Others, like Saro-Wiwa, detested the idea of Biafra and felt that their best bet for the future lay with Gowon and his twelve-state solution. Saro-Wiwa had a special personal animosity toward Ojukwu, whom he accused directly "of exploiting Ibo suffering for [his] private purposes and of destroying the community that was Eastern Nigeria."[9] The majority of non-Igbo in the east preferred to wait and see how Biafran secession would unfold. The fact that the minorities did not wholeheartedly commit to Biafra made them targets for the Biafran Civil Defence. However, the fact that they were from the Eastern Region made them yameri in northern eyes. As a result, they were targeted by both Nigeria and Biafra.

When the war erupted in June 1967, Saro-Wiwa was a graduate assistant at the University of Nigeria–Nsukka, which was quickly renamed the University of Biafra. He made plans to leave as soon as the fighting reached the city in early July. Saro-Wiwa was in a precarious position as an Ogoni who was vehemently against Biafra as a nation and against Ojukwu as a leader. However, he was trapped in Biafra and fled to Bane in the Ogoni homeland near Port Harcourt, where he remained until September.

In the summer of 1967, Biafran forces launched an assault across the River Niger and conquered the Midwestern Region in a lightning assault, renaming the territory the Republic of Benin. However, the small Biafran force, led by Banjo, could not hope to hold the vast territory it conquered. By the end of August, the Biafrans were ousted from the territories they held to the west of the Niger. More important, the Biafran offensive diverted both troops and attention from the south of the country, where at the end of July, the Nigerian navy and army launched the largest amphibious invasion conducted by an African military and captured the key oil depot at Bonny, at the easternmost mouth of the Niger Delta.

During this turmoil, Saro-Wiwa still worked to create some semblance of a life for himself. However, despite being a prolific writer, piecing together the story of his personal life during this period is no easy task. The bulk of his work consisted of fiction during his early career, and later in life he shifted to the polemic work that would leave his most lasting legacy. He wrote very little about his personal life, and he never mentioned his relationship with his wife, Maria, who was only seventeen years old when the war broke out and presumably when they married. He only mentioned her briefly in relating how they clandestinely fled Biafran territory. Their eldest son, Ken Wiwa, in his memoir *In the Shadow of a Saint* provides very little information except what his father had previously published; the only biographical information he provides is to confirm that he was born in 1968.

Immune from the euphoria engulfing Biafra in the summer of 1967, Saro-Wiwa made plans, along with Maria, to flee from his home in Bane to Bonny. Saro-Wiwa set out on the night of September 23, 1967, via canoe, as Bonny was reachable only via air or water, as it remains in 2016. The tributaries of the Niger Delta were constantly patrolled by both Nigerian and Biafran forces, adding to the trip's danger. Saro-Wiwa made the journey without incident and arrived in Bonny a few days later.

After being detained briefly in Bonny, Saro-Wiwa journeyed to Lagos and joined other activists from the Rivers region who were forming a government in exile for the newly created Rivers State. This group, which they named the Rivers State Study Group, influenced the Nigerian government to install the Rivers State government during the war. Saro-Wiwa was appointed civil administrator of Bonny. His return to the town was delayed for several months due to intense fighting, as the Biafrans attempted to retake the strategic oil facility.

When he finally arrived in January 1968, Saro-Wiwa found that the city had suffered tremendously from the fighting. Further, Bonny's economy, based on trade between the interior and coastal merchants since precolonial times, was virtually nonexistent. As a result, the city was entirely dependent on the military for living essentials, as it could be supplied only from Lagos. Saro-Wiwa immediately embarked on several programs to ensure that life in the city would be bearable until the war ended.

His first priority was to oversee the city's food distribution program, ensuring that the few supplies entering Bonny would be distributed equitably, and not hoarded by the entrenched trading families in the city to be resold at inflated prices. He reopened the schools in the area, which had been closed since the war began, and sent the more advanced students, who could not be taught in the city, to Lagos to continue their schooling.

As with any wartime frontline city, relations between the military and the civilians could occasionally turn tense. Saro-Wiwa used his rapport with both military and civilian officials to minimize the friction. One of the key commanders in the area, Colonel (later Lieutenant General) Ipoola Akinrinade, who became chief of army staff in 1979, became a lifelong friend.

Saro-Wiwa learned more than the basics of administrative work during his time in Bonny. More important, he laid the foundation of the Rivers State administration. Between January and the end of August 1968, when he left his post, the war turned decidedly in Nigeria's favor. His Ogoni homeland was liberated by the federal forces, followed shortly by the fall of Port Harcourt during May 17–24, 1968.

Saro-Wiwa's task was difficult, especially in light of the nature of modern warfare and the poisoned relationship between the different ethnic groups enmeshed in the Nigerian Civil War. Saro-Wiwa recalled several disturbing events in which federal troops were accused, not without evidence, of assaulting and humiliating civilians, stealing food and money, and rape. As administrator of Bonny, he chose not to pursue the matter after speaking to Colonel Akinrinade, who assured him that the accusations were false. In his memoirs, he wrote,

"What's rape in war time?"[10] When Saro-Wiwa returned to Bane, he discovered that his sister had gone into hiding to escape the "raping Federal troops," while Biafran forces singled out his family for special treatment because of his open support of Nigeria. The retreating Biafran troops burned his house and most of his documents and personal effects in a giant bonfire.

When federal forces took Port Harcourt, the largely abandoned city experienced unprecedented looting. Saro-Wiwa recalled seeing everything from kitchen utensils and radios to doors, windows, and air conditioning units arrive on ships from Port Harcourt into Bonny on the way to Lagos and other parts of Nigeria. Port Harcourt, as a predominantly Igbo city carved out by British colonial policies in non-Igbo territory, exemplified the problems of Nigeria like no other place. Igbo came to dominate the politics of the city, marginalizing the indigenous Ikwerre. When oil was discovered in the Ogoni region in 1957, Port Harcourt, along with Bonny, became an important center for the oil industry, inflating the town's population significantly.

The city turned into a veritable Igbo colony inside the Niger Delta. Located outside their traditional homeland, the city became a symbol of Igbo regional domination. When the war ended in 1970, the Igbo attempted to reclaim their place in the city and demanded reparations from the Rivers State government for the looting and abandoned property now occupied by those who remained. The new Rivers State administration sought to redress the hardships the war had wrought on the non-Igbo population by marginalizing the Igbo, who were a minority in the new state. For Niger Delta activists, the city was a symbol that imperialism did not have to be European. Africans had practiced the same type of domination toward one another since well before colonial times. Saro-Wiwa wrote that Nigerian domination of the Ogoni amounted to little more than "Nigerian domestic colonialism, a colonialism which is cruel, unfeeling and monstrous."[11]

His experiences implementing the government policies for the new Rivers State left Saro-Wiwa disheartened regarding the future of the country. Even after cooperating with the other groups from the Delta in creating the new state, what emerged was a political entity mirroring Nigeria as a whole, only with a new majority imposing its newfound power to settle old scores. Acknowledging his naïveté in later years, he saw how the Rivers State simply replicated the old structures of Nigeria, creating new internal powers, while perpetuating the victimhood of the Ogoni and other marginalized people, whom Saro-Wiwa hoped the new structure would protect.

The Nigerian Civil War raged on until January 1970. Despite losing Port Harcourt, the Igbo fought on, determined to resist what they claimed was a war of extermination. Though the Nigerian military continuously encircled the beleaguered enclave, the Biafrans fought until January 9, 1970, when Ojukwu fled the country for the Ivory Coast leaving his chief of staff, Philip Efiong, in command of Biafra. Almost immediately, Efiong signaled his intent to end the war, and the official surrender took place in Lagos when Gowon embraced him, symbolically welcoming the east back to Nigeria.

Saro-Wiwa's involvement in the war ended when the Rivers State was created. He assumed many posts in the new government, such as the commissioner for works, land, and transport and commissioner for the Ministry of Education in the state. He was also appointed to the executive council, a post he held until 1973 when he was removed for pressing Ogoni rights. Disillusioned, Saro-Wiwa left the Rivers State administration, moved to Port Harcourt and started his first business, which would become Saros International. This venture again transformed his life and legacy, both in Nigeria and abroad.

# 4

# Business, Writing, and Politics

Had Ken Saro-Wiwa never formed Movement for the Survival of the Ogoni People (MOSOP) or suffered his fate at the hands of Sani Abacha in 1995, he would most likely be celebrated as one of Nigeria's greatest literary figures alongside Chinua Achebe and Wole Soyinka. Saro-Wiwa first came to the world's attention in 1986, with the publication of *Sozaboy: A Novel in Rotten English*. This novel, written in a mixture of English and Nigerian pidgin, satirized the jingoism of the Nigerian Civil War and its effect on the ordinary people who, Saro-Wiwa contended, did not know what they were fighting for. The next year, his collection of short stories, *A Forest of Flowers*, was shortlisted for the Commonwealth Writers Prize. Saro-Wiwa's literary career, which included novels, short stories, plays, and television scripts, was both a means to earn a living and a way to show Nigerians a common culture transcending ethnicity, even in a country built on ethnic patronage networks.

Saro-Wiwa's humor shines through in his literary work, showing Nigerians as one people, even if they failed to see or agree with it. His television show, *Basi and Company,* which ran from 1985 to 1990 and was the single most popular program in Nigerian Television (NTV) history, used his biting sarcastic wit and humor to show situations that all Nigerians could relate to. His writing engaged the poverty, corruption, and mismanagement Nigerians saw every day, and his wit gave ordinary Nigerians, fearful of the consequences of open

**Figure 4.1** Ken Saro-Wiwa. Pencil drawing by Kazeem Oyetunde Ekeolu, 2015

discourse, an avenue to laugh at their predicament and to unify in recognition of suffering that was not specifically Ogoni, Igbo, Yoruba, or Hausa but as something that was uniquely Nigerian.

During the war and in its immediate aftermath, Saro-Wiwa established himself as a leader in the new Rivers State. He also established several businesses, including a short-lived transport company that consisted mainly of buses, a grocery store, and wholesale company, and most important, the publishing company Saros International. The publishing company would become synonymous with much of his work. In the early 1970s, Saro-Wiwa rapidly accumulated wealth owing in no small part to using his public office to enhance his private business interests. As a government official, he served in many capacities with overlapping responsibilities. For instance, from 1967 to 1973, he was on the payroll as an assistant lecturer at the University of Lagos. At the same time, from 1968 until 1969, he served in the Rivers State as commissioner for land, works, and transport. From 1969 until 1971 he was commissioner for the Ministry of Education in Rivers State, and until 1973 he was in the Ministry of Information.

While holding these posts, he organized several public/private partnerships, in one case licensing a series of school textbooks through Saros. As commissioner in the Department of Education, he assigned these textbooks as the required texts for the state schools. Similarly, his wholesale company, the Market Masters, secured the contract to supply daily meals at the Port Harcourt area schools.

More troubling was Saro-Wiwa's attitude regarding properties abandoned in Port Harcourt during the civil war. Most of the Igbo population fled the city when federal forces captured it in 1968. Many people from the Niger Delta occupied the deserted buildings and claimed ownership of them as spoils of war. Saro-Wiwa himself bought a property at 24 Aggrey Road in Port Harcourt very shortly after the war, which had previously been the home of Chief Z. C. Obi, who was a senator during the First Republic. In 1976, Olusegun Obasanjo, in one of his first actions as head of the Federal Military Government (FMG), attempted to settle disputes over ownership of these properties by returning many of them to their prewar owners. If this was not possible, he attempted to compel the occupiers of the properties to pay market value to the previous owners. Like many in Port Harcourt, Saro-Wiwa was incensed, accusing Obasanjo of abandoning his wartime allies. "I went to war with you without a catapult and I ended up as a shopkeeper and you came back with epaulets," he charged. "I have a distinct feeling that you want to leave me a shopkeeper forever." Obasanjo replied to the accusation, "I did not fight the war for the Igbos to lose their properties in Nigeria."[1]

In 1977, Obasanjo began the transition that culminated in the return to civilian rule in 1979. Saro-Wiwa, by then removed from his positions within the Rivers

State government, was running for election to a constitutional convention intended to dictate the terms for the 1979 elections and subsequent government. Saro-Wiwa's eldest son remembered the Election Day in 1977:

> Nineteen seventy-seven was the year something died in my father. . . . Elections to a constituent assembly that was to draw up a constitution for the new republic were held as part of the transition process. My father stood as the Ogoni candidate but was defeated by one vote. There were bitter accusations of election fraud, and in the recriminations my father fell out with his friend Edward Kobani.
>
> I remember watching the news as the results came in. When my father's defeat was announced, he turned to me with tears in his eyes. "What do you think about that?" he asked.
>
> I didn't know what to say. I was stunned, not just that he had lost, but because it was the first time I had seen my father cry. I shrugged and he returned to the news. He had expected to win, and the disappointment of losing that election left him with an abiding distaste for conventional politics.[2]

In the wake of his defeat, Saro-Wiwa sent his family to London in January 1978. In addition to Kenule Jr., who had been born in 1968, his second son Gian was born in 1970, followed by twins Noo and Zina in 1976, and Tedum in 1978, after the family's relocation to England. Tedum would die of a heart condition while playing sports at Eton in 1992, a devastating blow to the family.

After the 1977 election came Saro-Wiwa's most prolific writing phase, his first major legacy. Saros International became Saro-Wiwa's main publishing arm, and the main financial hub of his business ventures. Indeed, many of his nongovernmental activist organizations never had separate bank accounts; all monies went through Saros's accounts. This centralization of funding contributed to his enemies' grievances. Saro-Wiwa also used proceeds from his business ventures to subsidize much of his literary work. Many of his works garnered him a worldwide following, a fact that aided his later campaign to attract international attention to the tragedy brewing in the Niger Delta.

Saro-Wiwa's poetry showcases the rawest emotions he suffered during the war. These poems are some of his most personal works. Saro-Wiwa often included portions of his poetry in his polemical writings, and he wrote poetry profusely, though he published only one poetry collection, *Songs in a Time of War*. Most of his poems were wartime poetry and have some ghastly imagery illustrating the ravages of war:

> A lone lean dog
> Scrounging for food
> Reaps human skulls
> In a shallow gutter

Dogs, normally humans' companions, are reduced to eating the remains of the war's victims. This stanza, taken from a poem called "Ogale—An Evacuated

Town," also shows the empty houses, the "cannibalized" cars, and many other haunting images of a war that affected the author very deeply. Saro-Wiwa wrote most of the poems in the collection either during or soon after the end of the war. They showcase the dejection that Saro-Wiwa felt while immersed in a conflict he viewed as senseless.

Though he rarely returned to poetry after the initial burst of poems written in the civil war's aftermath, he wrote several poems in the years before his execution, several of which were published in his prison diary. In one, called "The True Prison," he lamented the predicament of his arrest and that of Nigeria as a whole, explaining the significance of being in prison not in terms of the physical confinement and squalid conditions he suffered, but

> It is the lies that have been drummed
> Into your ears for one generation
> It is the security agent running amok
> Executing callous calamitous orders
> In exchange for a wretched meal a day
> The magistrate writing in her book
> Punishment she knows is undeserved.[3]

His poetry showcases raw pain and emotion that rarely came across in his prose writing, for which he was much better known. The pain for his country exists in all his writing, but unlike in his poetry, his prose and screen writings mask the pain with a heavy dose of biting sarcasm, wit, and humor that he rarely expressed in his poetry, making his poetry both unique in his body of work and a window into the heart of what he saw as the tragedy of Nigeria.

Saro-Wiwa left a large body of work when he departed from the literary world in 1990. This legacy, combined with his journalistic prowess, saw a perfect combination in his serialized novel, *Prisoners of Jebs*. In the story, Jebs is the name of a fictional megaprison that the Organisation of African Unity (OAU) erects to house the worst criminals in Africa. Naturally, the OAU awarded the contract for building the prison to Nigeria. The prison, situated on an island, is built after corrupt government officials decide they can steal more money by building the prison than by not building it. The story revolves around the contradictions in the Nigerian rule of law and the application of that law to prisoners, many of whom end up having a hand in running the prison. The work serves as a satire on the nature of justice in a country ruled by a military elite with few scruples regarding the use and abuse of their power.

*Prisoners of Jebs* attacks Nigerian social structures from virtually every angle, in ways that are exaggerated yet familiar to people in the country. One example is the figure of the kangaroo: the kangaroo, head of the court responsible for sending so many prisoners to Jebs, eventually runs afoul of the regime he has loyally supported and ends up in Jebs himself. Saro-Wiwa also settles some personal scores in the story, especially with certain of his critics. Pita Dumbrok, a journalist character imprisoned for disagreeing with the government in print, is based on a journalist who criticized Saro-Wiwa's earlier works of fiction. Dumbrok's catchphrase, after he is placed in a gibbet, is "silly plot!" which is how the real-life journalist described Saro-Wiwa's work. Dumbrok, however, is useful in the story, not just as an ornament chirping about "silly plot." Despite his lack of sophistication, he serves as a voice for the people of Nigeria, often reacting to real life events with a mixture of pride, when Wole Soyinka wins the Nobel Prize, and pessimism, as when he learns that the journalist Dele Giwa was killed by a letter bomb, presumably sent by Ibrahim Badamasi Babangida's feared State Security Service (SSS).[4]

*Jebs* proved extremely popular in its serialized form and was eventually published in a single volume. The popularity of *Jebs*, like that of some of his later works, can be attributed to its prolific use of sardonic humor. By using humor to showcase Nigeria's woes, Saro-Wiwa let his readers laugh about their shared predicament under a government with little regard for its population. His humor eventually earned him a wide audience with his television series *Basi and Company.*

In his most critically celebrated work, *Sozaboy: A Novel in Rotten English,* published in 1985, Saro-Wiwa tells the story of a young, partially educated man in an unnamed African country faced with a civil war. Though the name of the country is never mentioned, the place names, such as Bori and Diobu, are indicative of Nigeria and, in particular, Ogoniland. The main protagonist, Mene, though he does not understand the reasons behind the war, eventually joins the secessionist military, in part to impress a woman who accused him of cowardice. The story develops along lines similar to those in *All Quiet on the Western Front*, questioning the jingoism and enthusiasm for war when the characters are faced with its bloody realities.

*Sozaboy* became internationally renowned, partly because of the innovative use of Nigerian pidgin. Because of this, it is one of the most studied of Saro-Wiwa's works. Saro-Wiwa states in the introduction that he took the risk of using dialect only because one of his professors at the University of Ibadan claimed that a credible work rooted in Nigerian pidgin could not be done. The resulting novel incorporates what some have termed the "management of what, at first, sound like the utterances of a demented mind."[5] Saro-Wiwa invented words that made sense to the characters' context, creating a new English dialect and "indigenizing" it, not to Nigerians, but to the characters of the book. One word in particular, "lomber," meaning number, is not a word in Standard English, but is also not immediately recognizable to speakers of Nigerian pidgin. Thus Saro-Wiwa created a pidgin unique to the book itself, with the characters almost organically adopting a language that made sense within the confines of Saro-Wiwa's fictional world.

The story's unique language may be viewed as a product of Nigeria's war experience. The innovative use of language serves to "arrest the reader's interest and provoke his/her consciousness about the evil, violence, destruction and other such negative influences of war on humanity."[6] One prominent example is when Mene, the lead character, meets a group of old men who fought during the Second World War. The old men recalled their service in Burma, where they fought the "hitlahs," boasting how many "hitlahs" they killed, thus showcasing their ignorance about the war they risked their lives fighting.

His collection of short stories, *A Forest of Flowers*, garnered him his first global exposure when it was shortlisted for the Commonwealth Book Prize in 1987. This collection was also quite innovative; in fact, "High Life," though published after *Sozaboy,* was written before it and was his first attempt at writing in the "broken English" that would later garner much critical acclaim for its use in *Sozaboy.* Saro-Wiwa's experimentation with the unique variations in Nigerians' English made "High Life" a unique piece, showcasing themes that recur throughout his work. The stories are split between urban and rural themes, and tackle many issues Nigerians have repeatedly encountered throughout the country's lifetime, both as a colonial possession and an independent nation. Saro-Wiwa's use of language, especially different vernaculars, highlights the different origins and educational background of the characters and stresses the tensions between different parts of society and the consequences of systemic institutional neglect in education, infrastructure, and other aspects of Nigerian society. Many grievances Saro-Wiwa enumerated in the Ogoni Bill of Rights first found their expression in his fiction, and much of that discussion occurred in *A Forest of Flowers,* some of it copied word for word to the Bill of Rights. However, although the images of poverty in the Bill of Rights are written as earnest illustrations of suffering intended to elicit sympathy, in the story "Home Sweet Home," economic underdevelopment is used for comedic effect, especially in the case of a rickety bus that is the pride of the village.[7]

Many stories in the collection feature women as both narrators and narrative subjects, an innovation that has been the subject of much critical analysis and acclaim. By using a female voice for many of the stories within the collection, Saro-Wiwa "confers on them a collective feminine identity. They become 'Everywoman,' the characters serving to embody aspects of the universal feminine." However, Saro-Wiwa's use of the feminine voice must also be acknowledged as a vehicle for "the author's male consciousness and its patriarchal construction of woman, thus coloring and contouring female experience with male gender perspectives."[8]

Though Saro-Wiwa received much critical acclaim for his books and poetry, arguably his most important work was the television program *Basi and Company.* The central character is Basi, or Mr B for short, a scheming huckster who has come to Lagos to get rich, played first by Albert Egbe and then by Zulu Adigwe. His goal in life, like that of many Nigerians, is to utilize the corruption in the system to get rich without actually working. His famous catchphrase is emblazoned on his red T-shirt, which reads on the front "MR B SAYS TO BE A MILLIONAIRE" and on the back "THINK LIKE A MILLIONAIRE."[9] The rest of the cast features equally unscrupulous but endearing characters like Madam, the landlady of the room he rents, and Mr B's lackey, Alali, who constantly complains of hunger.

The series tackles many complications of life in Nigeria, and in Lagos in particular. The action takes place on the fictional Adetola Street. Basi and his supporting cast are archetypical Lagosians in the eyes of most Nigerians. The self-centered, egotistical cheats engage in all sorts of schemes to avoid paying taxes and otherwise contribute to society. Basi himself justified his lack of civic responsibility by saying, "What do they use the tax for, anyway? There are no drugs in the hospital, the roads are full of potholes and the schools have no books. I won't pay my tax unless they supply all these things."[10] Basi and his friends also do their best to avoid bribes to the police, with Basi at one point even impersonating an officer to solicit bribes.

Most episodes address circumstances familiar to all Nigerians, irrespective of their ethnicity. In one episode, *Dead Men Don't Bite,* Basi hatches a scheme to fake his death in order to collect money from both Madam and his acquaintance Dandy, the owner of the local tavern.

As with most episodes, this begins with Alali pestering Basi about hunger. The pair realize that they are broke and have only a bag of tea, which Alali promptly eats. In the next scene, Basi begs Madam for three naira to buy food. Madam denies the request, because her social club, "The American Dollar Club," has just lost a member and she must contribute to the lavish funeral. Madam informs Basi that if he dies, she will fund an extravagant funeral for him, but he can expect no money from her in life.

Basi returns to the one-room apartment he shares with Alali, where Alali is reading the obituary for Basi's uncle who has recently passed away. Knowing that he will be expected to help pay for the funeral, Basi sends Alali to the tavern to ask Dandy for a loan. Dandy refuses, giving a response similar to Madam's, stating that he will happily pay for Basi's funeral, but that Basi is a wicked man and will get no money from him. When Basi leaves for his uncle's funeral, he fakes his death in a road accident and instructs Alali to collect the money from Madam and Dandy to pay for the funeral and disco party. The two donate over two thousand naira, and pay for the food, brandy, and entertainment at the funeral. However, Basi, lying as a corpse in the center of the room, cannot control himself and begins to move his feet to the music, betraying his ruse. Madam and Dandy immediately demand their money back, but Basi scolds them: "You refused to lend me three naira just to stave off hunger, but you were prepared to spend a

73

thousand times that amount on my funeral!" concluding that "what you gave me in death, I claim in life!" The episode ends with Basi repeating this catchphrase.

This episode, like many in the series, avoided ethnic stereotypes in favor of one that treated all ethnicities as Nigerians. Saro-Wiwa created the program to make it impossible to discern the ethnicities of the characters. Instead, he focused on themes common to all Nigerians, as in this episode where he tackled what he saw as the hypocrisy of funding extravagant death rites while refusing to help alleviate suffering in life. He also eschewed the colloquial and often localized pidgin English that was not always mutually understandable across the country in favor of a more standard language, one that could be understood by all Nigerians. Though the artistic merits were consistent with most low-budget productions anywhere in the world, the result was a national phenomenon that attracted worldwide attention on its social and political merits. In an interview with the *New York Times,* Saro-Wiwa and the series director, Uzorma Onungwa, explained how they purposefully wrote the program to avoid ethnic humor and show Basi as a microcosm of Nigeria. "I have used it to excoriate Nigerian society at the moment," Saro-Wiwa said in the interview. "Many rich Nigerians, especially of the political class, have the 'Basi' complex—they are hustling con men." Onungwa added, "We are trying to teach Nigerians that working hard really pays—not lazing around." Aso Ikpo-Douglas, who played Madam, sometimes lamented what she felt was the lost message of the show. She told the *Times*, "When I go to the market, the women immediately inflate the prices; they think I have all the millions in my bag. They don't know that in real life I don't have the money."[11]

Basi's antics secured Saro-Wiwa and his family more financial stability than most of his other literary work. With *Basi*, Saro-Wiwa created an iconic franchise for the first time and used Basi and his zany cohort as the core of a broad publishing enterprise. Along with the television series, Basi starred in novelizations of the show's episodes, with editions for both adults and students, as Saro-Wiwa had not forgotten his call to use his talent to educate. Every episode of the television show contained an advertisement for these novelizations and for Saro-Wiwa's others works, with purchasing information. When Saro-Wiwa briefly returned to the government in 1989 as head of the directorate of Mass Mobilization for Self Reliance (MAMSER), he used the post to sponsor the production of the show, undoubtedly for his own personal benefit. He also collected and sold the screenplays as books and created new adventures for his characters that went straight to the bookshelves without being produced for television.

Why Saro-Wiwa stopped writing creatively in 1990 has long been a subject of intense speculation. Saro-Wiwa once stated he was working on a manuscript that disappeared in a taxi, either misplaced or stolen, though his son recalls it happening at Murtala Mohammed airport in Lagos in 1992. Regardless of the exact circumstances, losing the manuscript prompted him to stop writing until he felt conditions obligated him to write *Genocide in Nigeria.* That story may be rather fanciful, as he did write some other important nonfiction texts in the interim, including the Ogoni Bill of Rights. Others point to the death of his son in 1992 as a turning point in his life, which drove him to dedicate himself to his people rather than to literature. Whatever the reason, after 1990 when *Basi and Company* ended its run on NTV, Saro-Wiwa never wrote creatively again, instead focusing his life on his activism on behalf of the Ogoni and the creation of the Movement for the Survival of the Ogoni People (MOSOP).

# 5

# Activism and the Politics of Oil, the Environment, and Genocide

Until 1973, Ken Saro-Wiwa worked within the Rivers State government. In 1973 he was sacked from his position for using government money to fund private business trips to the United Kingdom and the United States. After his removal from government, he dedicated himself to his business interests, which depended heavily on his contacts within government. Because of his loss in the election to the constitutional assembly, political machinations in Nigeria were distasteful to him. The loss of the election spurred him to return to his first professional love—literature. It was not until 1990, when he left the TV show *Basi and Company* and his editorial post, that he once again thrust himself into Ogoni politics, this time creating an outsider mass movement, MOSOP (Movement for the Survival of the Ogoni People), tapping into the collective anger and despair to combat more than twenty years of neglect, corruption, and environmental destruction. He dedicated the last five years of his life to this struggle.

The Niger Delta became crucial to the country as a whole in 1958 as commercial production of oil began and the region became the center of the new oil economy. Expansion of the petroleum industry in Nigeria accelerated after the Nigerian Civil War in 1970. The dependence on oil transformed Nigeria into a "rentier state," prioritizing the support of the oil sector's economic interests above maintaining a functioning and functional state apparatus.[1]

Saro-Wiwa quickly became one of the leading voices in the fight against resource exploitation in the Delta and the oppression of the Rivers people, following in the footsteps of Ogoni and Ijo activists such as Paul Birabi, who spent over half a century agitating for more local control over environmental stewardship.

As Saro-Wiwa portrayed in his writings and public commentaries, these changes profoundly affected the Ogoni. Like other riverine peoples in the region, the Ogoni depended on the fertile Niger Delta for every aspect of their livelihood. As he argued, the economic revolution manifested itself in two distinct yet intertwined ways. First, oil exploration and production devastated the Niger Delta's ecology, affecting every facet of life in the region. He pointed out that numerous oil spills, gas flarings, and pipeline failures caused environmental damage that poisoned waterways, killed the marine life that the local populations depended on for food, and rendered large parcels of land unusable for agriculture. This widespread environmental catastrophe sparked protests that were brutally suppressed by the Nigerian police and military, with help from Shell and other oil companies. As Saro-Wiwa pointed out, adding to the Ogoni misery, very little wealth extracted from the oil fields ever returned to the Ogoni in any form of government investment, as an increasingly corrupt Nigerian state diverted funds to other areas of Nigeria and into their own pockets. This state apparatus also increasingly guaranteed oil company rights and systematically dispossessed Ogoni farmland, requiring the oil companies to make only symbolic payments, which fell far short of reasonable compensation for the loss of the fertile agricultural lands.

Oil companies had searched for commercial quantities of oil in Nigeria since the early twentieth century. The first oil discovery came in November 1908, during the first petroleum exploration in the country at Lekki Lagoon, on the eastern edge of modern-day Lagos State. Nigeria Bitumen, the first company to prospect for oil, made this discovery but could not prevent water seepage into the oil field due to technological constraints; this negated their ability to produce oil in commercial quantities. This first discovery was also the first recorded case of an oil spill in Nigeria. Nigeria Bitumen's manager, Frank Drader, wrote to his wife expressing his disappointment that the oil well would not be economically feasible, stating casually that "the lagoon is at present all covered with oil . . . and there was so much oil at our wharf here that the Doctor got all covered last night when he went in swimming, which he does every evening."[2] This spill foreshadowed the decades of environmental impact that the Niger Delta suffered at the hands of the oil industry when exploration and production penetrated the region.

The impact of commercial drilling in the Ogoni region in 1958 was clearly multifaceted and profound. Saro-Wiwa's civil war experiences saw him placed in a central position as commissioner for education in the new Rivers State. He addressed many of the region's issues in his 1992 polemic *Genocide in Nigeria: The Ogoni Tragedy*.[3] This work chronicles the antecedents that led him to his struggle for the Ogoni people, detailing the links between the plight of the Ogoni, the systematic dispossession of their homeland, and the poisoning of the environment. In particular, he noted the collusion between the government and the oil industry that disregarded the massive pollution and collaborated in the dispossession of land for drilling purposes.

Access to land quickly became a major point of contention for oil companies and the government. Before 1977, oil companies had to negotiate with landowners to obtain the rights to prospect and drill. As a result of the Nigerian National Petroleum Corporation (NNPC) oil payment structure, land access rights provided local communities with some leverage against the oil companies. In fact, landowners sometimes succeeded in either blocking government seizure of the land or obtaining significant compensation. In one landmark case, a family leased land to Shell in 1957 on a ninety-nine-year lease. Shell agreed to pay the family GBP 945 per year. However, in 1960, the Nigerian government proposed a new lease that would cut the payments to GBP 20 per year. The family sued the government and was awarded GBP 252,600 for their land. In 1978 the government enacted the Land Use Act to restrict such appeals. The Land Use Act of 1978 gave the state governor rights to lease all lands in the state determined to be of "overriding public interest," with a special stipulation listed in section 28 for the "the requirement of the land for mining purposes or oil pipelines or for any purpose connected therewith."[4] Even worse for landowners, all payments for the land went directly to the governor and not to the landowners or the local communities. The law required that the landowners and local communities had to be compensated only for the destruction of improvements to the land. However, all payments for these compensations were also disbursed to the governor, who could then decide whether to transfer the payments to the afflicted party. Most damaging, the 1978 law revoked the owners' ability to use the court system: section 30 stated that "any dispute as to the amount of compensation calculated in accordance with the provisions of section 29 [which enumerated what is to be compensated], such dispute shall be referred to the appropriate Land Use and Allocation Committee." Interestingly, the Land Use Act came into effect a year before the transition to civilian rule in 1979, enacted by a lame duck military government hoping to ingratiate itself with the petroleum industry.

By 1970, the living situation in the Ogoni region had deteriorated to the point that a group of Ogoni leaders, among them Edward Kobani and W. Z. P. Ndizee (who would later side with Saro-Wiwa when crafting the Ogoni Bill of Rights twenty years later), drafted a petition detailing the hardships that Shell's activities had inflicted on the Ogoni. This group appealed to the military governor of the newly created Rivers State, cataloging the damages that could be directly attributed to Shell's activities. The letter, dated April 25, 1970, requested an interview with the governor to discuss environmental degradation in the Niger Delta and the direct impact Shell's operations had on the livelihoods of the Ogoni. It was clear that in the twelve years Shell had operated in the Ogoni region, the environmental and economic damage was making life untenable. In particular, the Ogoni leaders pointed to the degradation of the region's ability to produce food and Shell's active destruction of crops as direct results of the company's operations in the area. The Ogoni accused Shell of making payments of less than GBP 2 per acre of land to the landowners, who then could not cultivate their land, depriving them of between GBP 1,000–2,000 per annum. The Ogoni leaders also remarked on the destruction of crops, pollution of waterways, contamination of soil, and the degradation of infrastructure. The rudimentary roadways, originally built to accommodate local traffic, were now subjected to frequent use by the heavy machinery serving the oil fields, rendering the roads unusable during the rainy seasons. Years later Saro-Wiwa built on this case when crafting both the Ogoni Bill of Rights and *Genocide in Nigeria,* incorporating the ideas of the 1970 letter. In *Genocide in Nigeria* he fully developed his argument that all the environmental damage, coupled with the Nigerian State's actions, amounted to genocide.

Saro-Wiwa was not one of the signatories of the Ogoni letter, but he was a named a recipient in his capacity as the commissioner for education of Rivers State. This letter received no reply from the government. Shell, however, replied after two months, denying the allegations and stating that Shell's positive economic activity in the region far outweighed any detriment to a few farmers. Shell also accused the authors of presenting exaggerated claims in an effort to extract concessions

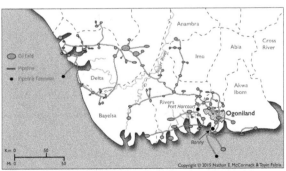

**Map 5.1** Ogoniland within the oil fields and pipelines of the Niger Delta

from the company, "which do not lie within its province or responsibilities."[5]

Almost as though predicted, on July 19, 1970, three months after the Ogoni leadership sent their petition to the Rivers State governor, one of the most devastating oil spills in Nigerian history occurred at the Bomu oil field in the heart of Ogoni. There, an array of valves used to regulate wellhead pressure, called a "Christmas tree," ruptured. The resulting spill continued unabated for three weeks. The spill wreaked havoc on the surrounding area, flooding up to a three-mile radius of the spill with crude oil, destroying crops, and contaminating fields. Even worse, the oil polluted the water supply up to eight miles away, polluting the creeks and killing the marine life people depended on for food. Shell went to great lengths to stop the flow of oil but prioritized the recovery of salable escaped crude over cleanup and recovery assistance to local communities. In fact, when Shell agreed to send adjustors to survey the damage, the company agreed to compensate the victims only for losses to crops and not for the damage done to the land that would affect future crop cycles. Ogoni residents refused to cooperate under these terms, stating, "Greater damage was also done to land and soil, drinking water, fishing ground, villages and air."[6] Shell made no move to remove the oil from the infected streams and rivers because this oil was no longer economically viable, and the Nigerian government did not extend any aid to the afflicted areas. It was only thirty years later, in 2000, that a Port Harcourt court fined Shell GBP 26 million for the spill. As a comparison, three years before the Bomu spill, a BP oil tanker, the *Torrey Canyon,* shipwrecked off the coast of Cornwall in southern England, spilling an estimated 32 million gallons of crude oil. In that case, the British government recouped GBP 3 million from BP after seizing another ship belonging to the company until the funds were paid.[7] In Nigeria, the spills that began in 1970 only became more frequent through the decades. In a 2006 report, the United Nations Development Programme (UNDP) estimated that as much as 350,000 tons of oil spilled in the Niger Delta between 1976 and 2001, most of which went unrecovered.[8]

Indeed, between 1970 and 2000, the Niger Delta and the Ogoni endured unrelenting suffering. The scale and scope of oil spills in the Delta are staggering. Between 1976 and 1996, seven thousand reported spills flooded the region with over two million barrels of oil; 77 percent of the lost oil became immersed in the soil and waterways. These spills were the result of both oil industry negligence and third parties rupturing pipelines to steal oil. The thefts are often especially horrific. The ruptured pipelines can explode, killing scores of people as they flock to collect oil for themselves. Since the late 1990s, several occurrences of this type have been reported. The single most devastating incident came in 1998 at Jesse, some 60 kilometers south of Benin City, where at least seven hundred people died, though some sources estimated as many one thousand two hundred or more were killed. Many victims reportedly feared reprisals from the government should they receive treatment and thus claimed to have sustained their injuries elsewhere.

In addition to the spills, gas flaring has been a constant threat both to the Niger Delta's environment and to global atmospheric quality. Gas flaring is a process by which natural gas that is trapped in oil reserves is siphoned through a tower and burned off. Because oil is more valuable than gas, many oil companies prefer to remove the gas that impedes oil production and causes hazardous situations for production rather than capture it for consumption or reinject it into the soil, both of which cost much more than simply burning the excess gas. Whereas most countries prohibit gas flaring except in emergencies, in the Niger Delta most of the gas is flared rather than captured. In 2002, the World Bank estimated that gas flaring in the Niger Delta amounted to 16 percent of the world's gas flaring and cost the Nigerian economy $2.5 billion annually both in damages and in lost revenue from the gas. The fires that rage day and night have created a hellish landscape all across the Niger Delta. The fires cause many health problems for Delta residents, ranging from systematic insomnia caused by the bright flares at night and the deafening roar of the raging fires to respiratory diseases from the emissions.

As a result of the gas flaring, many Delta food crops have been harmed by the emissions. Recent studies have shown that the quantity and quality of cassava roots decline the closer the cultivation is to flaring points. One study in the Eleme region confirmed that most crops suffer immensely due to proximity to gas flaring sites, with the only exception being the waterleaf (the main ingredient in gbure soup), which thrives on the elevated temperatures and appears immune to the released toxins.[9]

One Niger Delta resident summed up his plight dealing with both the oil spills and the gas flaring: "I left my town, Ughelli, because oil spills destroyed my farmland. I am now here in Ubeji [part of Warri], and the heat and toxins from gas flares are 'cooking' me up."[10] These environmental issues have placed a great strain on traditional riverine societies, including, but not limited to, the Ogoni. The environmental catastrophe disrupted many basic necessities of life and society in the Niger Delta. The oil companies, with Shell leading the way, became a sort of bubble economy in the region, driving up prices for basic commodities while disconnecting themselves from the local population's welfare. Most residents in the oil areas saw little benefit from the boom. Practically all revenues from oil were distributed to other parts of Nigeria, with a paltry 1.5 percent returning to the region for reinvestment as part of a derivation (or source) program discussed later in this chapter. The oil companies' engagement with most of the people in the region was minimal, mostly limited to employment as semi- and unskilled labor.

Many people in the area, unable to make a living because of drilling activity, moved to urban areas of Nigeria, usually to areas that were already overcrowded, leading to increased stress on urban centers such as Port Harcourt, Lagos, and Onitsha. These new migrations strained both the ability of people to cope with the dense population and the capacity of public services to provide health and social support. Several authors have noted the outcome of the increased strain. V. T. Jike of Delta State University stated the problem succinctly, "The migrant finds himself in a vicious cycle, unable to find a means of livelihood in the rural area, unable to realize his aspirations in his new urban abode and crammed in a little room with others in a similar plight."[11] This communal misery had a radicalizing social effect and spurred various Delta groups to organize in opposition to the oil companies and the Nigerian government that enabled the destruction of their lives.

If the environmental degradation and the dispossession of land created a an unbearable situation for the Ogoni, Saro-Wiwa assailed a pattern of systemic institutionalized corruption, economic centralization, and mismanagement diverting funds that could have helped alleviate these problems as the nail in the Ogoni coffin. "Political structuring and revenue allocation have been used to completely marginalize the Ogoni," Saro-Wiwa bluntly stated, "grossly abusing their rights and veritably consigning them to extinction."[12]

This pattern began in the colonial period, due in no small part to the British government's insistence that the oil industry be instrumental in Nigeria's economic future after independence. The British government attempted to implement several laws and ordinances, stating these were critical to ensure that at least some of the revenue would remain in Nigeria and benefit local governments. These measures were widely protested, as nationalist leaders, led by Azikiwe, saw the measures as little more than a veiled attempt to maintain British control over the resources after independence. Through a series of protests, Azikiwe secured more Nigerian control over the revenue, but not at the local level. The oil industry and its revenues would be tightly under national, not regional, control.[13]

This evolution of central control continued after independence and intensified after the civil war. In 1971, Yakubu Gowon's government created the Nigerian National Oil Company (NNOC). This government company managed relations between the Nigerian government and the large multinational corporations (MNCs) doing business in the country, including Shell, the Italian oil company ENI, and Mobil (later Exxon-Mobil). The NNOC also managed distribution of oil revenue around the country. The oil-producing regions agitated for a system of allocation based on the oil's source, or derivation. Leaders in areas of the country with no oil argued for a distribution based on population. In the end, a compromise led to 45 percent of the revenue going directly to the region of derivation, and 55 percent allocated to the federal government in the Distributable Pool Account (DPA). Because the NNOC and the Ministry of Mines and Power shared the DPA, the Obasanjo military government merged the entities into the NNPC in 1977 and reduced regional allocations to 20 percent before eliminating them entirely in 1979.

Population now solely determined regional access to oil funds, and corruption was rampant in the 1973 census, the first after the civil war. When Gowon ordered the census, he touted it as part of his plan to restore civilian rule, but results were greatly misrepresented, as the different states sought to receive a greater percentage of the DPA. Results showed Nigeria's population had risen 43 percent since the already exaggerated 1963 census and after a civil war that claimed at least one million lives.

Saro-Wiwa saw the ecological destruction as an insurmountable obstacle for the Ogoni. He thrust himself into a prominent leadership role, setting himself on a direct collision course with established Ogoni leaders, such as Kobani. Furthermore, Saro-Wiwa's work dramatically shifted the stakes in the conflict over the Niger Delta's resources. Most significantly, Saro-Wiwa's accusation, mentioned earlier, that Shell's destruction of the Delta and the government's complicity in that devastation amounted to genocide brought about a furious governmental response, supported by the oil giant, that led to multiple arrests and ultimately to his execution in 1995.

Corruption was not confined simply to access to funds. Federal coffers were awash with cash because of the rapid rise of oil prices after Nigeria joined OPEC. In 1974, two military officers, Joseph Gomwalk, governor of Benue-Plateau State, and the state's elections commissioner, Joseph Tarka, were both implicated in corruption schemes. Though Tarka resigned his post over the allegations, Gowon did not act on the charges and allowed Gomwalk to continue as governor. When Gowon declared he was delaying the transition to civilian rule indefinitely, Murtala Mohammed led a successful coup to overthrow him. Subsequent investigations revealed the depths of corruption in Gowon's regime: inquiries into the assets of Gowon's officials, including Gomwalk, revealed that only two of the twelve military state governors did not use state funds for personal enrichment. Gomwalk was subsequently executed, not for corruption, but for involvement in a retaliatory coup attempt against Mohammed's regime in 1976. Tarka returned to politics and was elected senator when Obasanjo returned the country to civilian rule in 1979, but he died a year into his term.

Gowon's regime also misappropriated funds to expand the military. At the end of the civil war in 1970, military expenditure totaled the equivalent of NGN 314.5 million in Nigerian pounds. In 1974, that sum had risen to NGN 1.116 billion. The goal of this expansion was not national security, but the securing of the military's loyalty. In addition, Gowon instituted salary increases to the civil service. In 1972, Gowon appointed Jerome Udoji to head a commission to review the civil service. Two years later, the commission made a series of recommendations that included the restructuring of the civil service, updating training regimes, elimination of waste by unifying divisions within the civil service, establishing a national ombudsman, and significant salary increases. Only the salary increases were ever implemented, mockingly referred to today as the "Udoji award."[14]

Infrastructure and building projects also contributed to vast mismanagement of funds. In 1966, the United Nations Educational, Scientific and Cultural Organization (UNESCO) sponsored the World Festival of Negro Arts (in French this was Festival mondial des arts nègres, or FESMAN) in Dakar, Senegal. Not to be outdone, Gowon sponsored, with UNESCO, a second festival in Lagos in 1977 called the Second World Black and African Festival of Arts and Culture (FESTAC 77). Gowon ordered a large development project built on the western outskirts of Lagos, called Festac Town, to accommodate the festival. The houses in this development were later given to government loyalists. Although Gowon was overthrown in 1975, both the Murtala Mohammed and Obasanjo regimes continued to pour money into the venture. This project set the stage for later military dictators and public officials to build lavish estates for their loyalists, one of the most opulent being the Abacha Estate that Sani Abacha built in the posh Lagos neighborhood of Ikoyi.[15]

Perhaps Gowon's most egregious misuse of funds came to be known as the "cement armada." In the summer of 1975, Gowon ordered significant upgrades to the military, including the construction of massive new barracks. Gowon announced the importation of 16 million tons of cement for 1975, quadruple the entire yearly import capacity for the country. Predictably, the port in Lagos became overburdened, creating gridlock in the shipping lanes as ships waited for dock space. However, the Gowon regime was so generous with demurrage fees that many ships arrived in Lagos just to wait in the queue to collect those fees. Later investigations revealed that the amount of cement was much in excess of what was necessary, because contractors inflated their bids in an attempt to defraud the government of as much money as possible. In fact, with so much money to spend and so little oversight on expenditures, virtually every infrastructure project was rife with theft and embezzlement on all levels, one of the hallmarks of a rentier state.

The 1980s and 1990s saw the collapse of the first attempt to return Nigeria to civilian rule. In 1979, Obasanjo orchestrated an attempt at transition, known as the Second Republic. Shehu Shagari, a northern Fulani Muslim with ancestral ties to the Sokoto Caliphate, presided over deepening corruption in the country. Shagari's corruption, coupled with a fall in the price of oil in the early 1980s led to economic stagnation and discontent among the different ethnic and religious groups in the country. In 1980, a large-scale religious rebellion led by Mohammed Marwa, known popularly as the Maitatsine, erupted throughout northern Nigeria. Though Maitatsine himself was killed in the city of Kano in 1980 along with nearly five thousand people in an intraurban civil war, many of his followers fled to the northeastern city of Maiduguri, where they continued their uprising until it was finally suppressed in April 1985. The total death toll of the Maitatsine revolt has been estimated from seven to ten thousand victims.[16]

After widespread allegations of election fraud in the 1983 federal elections, Major-General Muhammadu Buhari overthrew Shagari's government on December 31, 1983, and instituted a regime that achieved a level of brutality unseen before in Nigeria. His successors, Ibrahim Babangida and Sani Abacha, elevated theft and embezzlement to unheard-of proportions, even by the standard of previous military regimes. Both men, but especially Abacha, ruthlessly stifled any opposition. Saro-Wiwa's dealings with both of these regimes are discussed in the next two chapters.

**Figure 5.1** Cars queuing for petrol in Lagos during a strike, 2007

Corruption continued unabated after the transition to civilian rule in 1999 and has remained endemic in the Nigerian political system since. Several high-profile governors were implicated in corruption scandals. In 2007, 170 charges of money laundering, theft of public funds, and abuse of office were brought against James Ibori, governor of Delta State. Nuhu Ribadu, then head of the Economic and Financial Crimes Commission (EFCC), claimed Ibori attempted to "gift" him USD 15 million to drop the charges. When the case came to trial in December 2009, the Federal High Court acquitted Ibori of all charges. In 2010, after Goodluck Jonathan became president, the government filed new charges alleging that Ibori had embezzled USD 266 million. Ibori promptly fled Nigeria to Dubai. From Dubai, he was extradited to the United Kingdom, where Scotland Yard had been pursuing a case against him since 2007 for the same money-laundering allegations for which he was acquitted in the Nigerian courts in 2009. In February 2012, Ibori pled guilty and shortly thereafter began a twelve-year sentence in the United Kingdom.

Ibori's case was by no means unique. Diepreye Alamieyeseigha, governor of Bayelsa State, faced money-laundering charges in Nigeria, the United Kingdom, and the United States. While under investigation in the United Kingdom in 2005, he posted bail and fled the country with forged papers, reportedly disguised as a woman to avoid detection. In 2007, Alamieyeseigha pled guilty to six charges in Nigeria and was sentenced to two years for each charge. However, the court specified that all sentences were to run concurrently, and shortened his sentence to a matter of hours, due to time already served. In 2013, Goodluck Jonathan, Alamieyeseigha's deputy governor and successor as governor of Bayelsa State, pardoned Alamieyeseigha, a move that sparked much public outrage.

Corruption in the oil sector itself remained a problem for Nigeria as late as 2013. In November of that year Nigeria's Central Bank governor, Sanusi Lamido Sanusi, warned Jonathan that between January 2012 and July 2013 the Nigerian oil industry produced crude oil totaling royalties of USD 65 billion. Of that amount, only USD 15 billion were deposited, as required, with the NNPC. Sanusi accused the NNPC of failing to account for 76 percent of oil revenues. In response, the Nigerian government removed Sanusi from his post in February 2014, charging him with financial recklessness and fraud. Sanusi had been named the world's Central Banker of the Year in 2011 due to his anticorruption work.

Nigeria's political structure made opposition to the oil companies extremely difficult and perilous. Nevertheless, protests against the government began even before oil was discovered, and in some instances the protests prevented the oil companies from surveying prospective drill sites. Though most of these protests were unsuccessful, they were enough to force the British colonial administration to negotiate with Shell on behalf of the people. In 1951 the colonial government managed to gain several concessions that benefited the Nigerian population. Most important, the company agreed to place Nigerian subjects in senior levels of corporate administration. Unfortunately, the indigenization process was extremely slow, and by 1954 the company had only three Nigerians in senior positions. With the beginning of commercial production at Oloibiri, Shell and the other companies entering the market shifted their focus from other regions and attempted the first large-scale incursions into the Niger Delta. These incursions were limited by the existing laws that the oil companies had to adhere to, and despite the Nigerian administration's best efforts to acquiesce to the oil companies' demands, the courts continued to address people's grievances. However, once the First Republic collapsed in the January 1966 coup, the protections the court system afforded eroded, as the courts increasingly became mere tools for government oppression. This process led some groups in the Niger Delta to advocate violence and secession. Saro-Wiwa always supported a single Nigeria; he never advocated secession of any kind and preferred mass action and nonviolent resistance. However, the circumstances behind many of Saro-Wiwa's predecessors' actions were depressingly similar to those that led Saro-Wiwa to create MOSOP and agitate for Ogoni rights.

In the wake of the January 1966 coup, before Colonel Chukwuemeka Ojukwu planned his secession from Nigeria and opened the door to the Nigerian Civil War, a group of Ijo activists formed the Niger Delta Volunteer

Service (NDVS). According to their leader, a former policeman named Isaac Adaka Boro, they gathered a force of young men, telling the recruits they intended to express their dissatisfaction with the military government. However, Adaka Boro's real goal, which he hid from his recruits, was to "break the Niger Delta Area away into a nation and strive to maintain it."[17] The group began its activities in late January by intercepting illicit gin runners, but it also stockpiled weapons and on February 22, 1966, launched an assault on the town of Yenagoa, in modern-day Bayelsa State. After capturing the city, another NDVS force, led by Samuel Owonaru, attacked the Shell installation at Oloibiri and destroyed a portion of the Ughelli–Port Harcourt oil pipeline. Although oil exploitation was not one of the main grievances that the NDVS had with the Nigerian government, the oil facilities were attractive targets. This tactic backfired, as the threat to oil production spurred Ironsi's regime to quick action, and the revolt was quelled in less than two weeks.

In later years, Owonaru claimed the revolt was indeed driven by the lack of regional development precipitated by the siphoning of oil revenue from the Delta region. In an interview with the *Vanguard,* he stated:

> Realising that virtually all the resources were from
> our area, we felt the solution was armed struggle,
> even though we did not have enough resources when
> we adopted that military option. It's now history
> that we were put down easily by the federal might

and, for that, we were arrested, tried for treason and condemned to death in 1966 by the Ironsi regime.[18]

The group was imprisoned and sentenced to death for treason; however, after Gowon created the federal system in 1967, he pardoned Adaka Boro and his group on August 4, 1967. They joined the federal side in the civil war, with Adaka Boro stating in his memoirs that "I could not resist the joy of the fact that I was still alive to see the Rivers State created, thereby vindicating and justifying my stand."[19] Adaka Boro was killed in action in the battle for the Rivers State in 1968. Echoing Saro-Wiwa's stance during the civil war, the creation of a state gave Adaka Boro and the Ijo group the representation that would help eliminate the power imbalances that had plagued Nigeria since its inception.

This was the dangerous arena that Ken Saro-Wiwa entered in 1990 in which he eventually lost his life. Most fatal was his contention that the ecological disaster the oil companies and the Nigerian government inflicted on the Ogoni was tantamount to genocide. The next chapters chronicle how Saro-Wiwa positioned himself as a leader of the Ogoni, and the evolution of his view of Ogoni genocide.

# 6

# MOSOP, the Ogoni Bill of Rights, and Saro-Wiwa's Activism

When Ken Saro-Wiwa devoted himself entirely to the Ogoni cause, he did so because of his need to become, as he put it, *l'homme engagé.* This need to become a political man of action led Saro-Wiwa on a path that disrupted his business dealings, editorial writings, and television production. In 1990, his "Similia" column in the *Lagos Sunday Times* was unceremoniously axed after the Ibrahim Badamasi Babangida regime became angered by his writing. His time as the creator of *Basi and Company* also ended. In *Genocide in Nigeria,* he commented on his reasons for dedicating himself to the Ogoni struggle, stating that since the civil war, "I have watched helplessly as [the Ogoni] have been ground to dust by the combined effort of the multinational oil company, Shell Petroleum Development Company, the murderous ethnic majority in Nigeria and the country's military dictatorships."[1] After 1990, Saro-Wiwa published no further creative work, instead focusing his life on the project that eventually caused his execution: his activism on behalf of the Ogoni and the creation of the Movement for the Survival of the Ogoni People (MOSOP).

Saro-Wiwa faced several distinct yet interrelated problems in bringing the Ogoni plight to the country's attention and to global awareness. First, he had to face his old political foes within the Ogoni movement: Kenneth Kobani, who had opposed him in his election bid in 1977, and others who viewed any attempt at creating a mass movement as a direct challenge to their leadership. Second, he had to learn how use navigate the global activist networks and make his voice heard around the world. This was no easy feat, considering that the Ogoni were a minuscule minority in the Niger Delta, an area long neglected by human rights groups and environmental activists. Even more dangerous, he risked reprisals from the military government if he brought global scrutiny to the oil industry, the government's main source of revenue.

Though Saro-Wiwa was already a prominent global figure because of his writings and the attention that his television show had attained around the world, he had to quickly learn an entirely new language to communicate his message to the various NGOs specializing in human rights and environmental activism. Saro-Wiwa quickly learned to focus this message to link environmental destruction with genocide. In particular, he formulated an argument that the environmental damage done to the Ogoni homeland constituted indirect genocide, as it made conditions unlivable and destroyed the ability of the Ogoni to live as a society. This narrative resonated in Nigeria and reverberated around the world, giving Saro-Wiwa a global platform that ultimately led the military dictatorship to act with extreme brutality against him.

Saro-Wiwa's first order of business was to announce his platform and create an organization to lead the struggle against Shell's exploitation of Ogoniland. After publishing *On a Darkling Plain* in 1989, he was elected president of the Ogoni Central Union, an organization he created, where he organized a series of seminars on all aspects of Ogoni life, including the environmental devastation that had occurred since 1970. He recruited young activists and the old Ogoni political functionaries into an organization uniting all the factions and king-doms with the Ogoni into a unified single front, called the Movement for the Survival of the Ogoni People (MOSOP). In MOSOP, Saro-Wiwa created an organiza-tion that, though inspired by his work and personality, mobilized the hundreds of thousands of Ogoni.

Saro-Wiwa's creation of MOSOP and his achieve-ment of at least nominally unifying the different factions within the Ogoni leadership have been a matter of some controversy. Ken Wiwa, writing in his memoir *In the Shadow of a Saint*, described MOSOP as largely his father's own creation, stating, "Few people took much no-tice when he announced his intention to set up MOSOP. Nigerians love their acronyms. . . . Some of them, like the beleaguered NEPA (Nigerian Electrical Ports Author-ity [*sic*; actually National Electric Power Authority]) are national institutions, but most of them are anonymous, shadowy organizations with impressive looking initials that signify nothing."[2] Indeed, NEPA's lack of ability to supply power and its infamous corruption in collecting revenue were publicly ridiculed by the legendary Afrobeat drummer Tony Allen, who interpreted the acronym to mean Never Expect Power Always. When NEPA changed its name to the Power Holding Company of Nigeria (PHCN) in 2006, Nigerians quickly adapted, rebranding the new acronym to mean Please Hold Candles Now. The citizenry regarded any new organization as just another similarly empty acronym.

Saro-Wiwa himself gave credit to the established Ogoni leadership in MOSOP's creation, as they are all signatories to the Ogoni Bill of Rights and authors of several of the addendums to the document. Though Saro-Wiwa credited the established Ogoni political elites as partners to MOSOP's creation in his prison diary, published in 1995, this was likely an attempt to heal the rift between himself and the elders. The murder of several elders was the catalyst for Saro-Wiwa's eventual execution. He even stated in the diary that the organization's name was chosen in a meeting held at Kobani's home. However, Saro-Wiwa himself was the driving force behind the creation of the mass movement that MOSOP became. Although MOSOP was the most public of Ogoni organizations, Saro-Wiwa created several more, placing himself or those close to him at their heads. In addition to MOSOP, Saro-Wiwa created the Ogoni Central Union and two social clubs: Kagote, for Ogoni elites, and the Ogoni Klub, envisioned as a way to mobilize Ogoni youth. Through these organizations Saro-Wiwa became one of the major leaders of the Ogoni movement almost overnight, much to the chagrin of the established elders. To give his organization even more gravitas, Saro-Wiwa linked the Ogoni to the other minorities in Nigeria through an organization called the Ethnic Minority and Indigenous Rights Organization of Africa (EMIROAF) that he also created. The goal of this organization was to amplify and legitimize Saro-Wiwa's ability to speak on minority rights in Nigeria and abroad. The fact that Saro-Wiwa created MOSOP practically single-handedly led to major difficulties within the Ogoni leadership once the movement came to prominence after 1993.

With the Ogoni Bill of Rights, MOSOP announced its arrival on the Nigerian political scene. Although Saro-Wiwa and his fellow MOSOP leaders affirmed several times in the document that they were by no means separatists, the document they submitted to the Babangida government on October 2, 1990, challenged the existing power structure in Nigeria, particularly in the Niger Delta. The document was released and rereleased several times with various additions, including "An Appeal to the International Community" and a foreword that Saro-Wiwa penned on Christmas Eve 1991.

In the document, Saro-Wiwa reiterated his belief that the future of the Ogoni lay only within Nigeria, but that the Ogoni wished to have a larger say in how their affairs were conducted. The appeal in the Bill of Rights begins with twenty points of contention showing how the Ogoni were conquered and systematically marginalized, politically and economically, by both the British colonial administration and the Nigerian government. The document points to the forced integration of the Ogoni into Nigeria and their marginalization in a political structure minimizing their ability to control their own destiny. Despite their protests, as point 6 argues, they were included in the new Rivers State in 1967, a state consisting of several ethnic nationalities with differing cultures, languages, and aspirations.[3]

The document also touches on the economic marginalization that the Ogoni have suffered:

> 9. That in over 30 years of oil mining, the Ogoni nationality have provided the Nigerian nation with a total revenue estimated at over 40 billion Naira (N40 billion) or 30 billion dollars.

> 10. That in return for the above contribution, the Ogoni people have received NOTHING.

The group argued that the Ogoni had no running water, no electricity, and few opportunities for jobs at any level of the government. Although these points are cogent, these conditions had long been typical for the majority of people in the country. However, the environmental catastrophe in the Niger Delta region and the Ogoni area in particular was unlike anything else in Nigeria.

The original document, signed by practically the entire leadership of the Ogoni community, including Saro-Wiwa's main rivals in the leadership, demanded political autonomy for the Ogoni. MOSOP insisted that only through autonomy would the Ogoni be able to protect their lands, their people, and their culture. Quoting Awolowo, the Ogoni stated that "in a true federation, each ethnic group, no matter how small, is entitled to the same treatment as any other ethnic group, no matter how large." As a result, they demanded full rights over the economic future of Ogoniland, including the oil rights: "The right to the control and use of a fair proportion of Ogoni economic resources for Ogoni development" and "the right to protect the Ogoni environment and ecology from further degradation."[4]

The Babangida government did not respond to the Bill of Rights, but the government's next moves affirmed that they had read the document. The Babangida regime further Balkanized Nigeria into thirty states in 1991, taking care to keep the Ogoni annexed to a Rivers State dominated by the Ijo. Later, in 1996, Abacha created five new states, splitting the new Bayelsa State off from Rivers State, but taking care to leave the Ogoni in the same marginal position they continue to hold as of 2016. Saro-Wiwa and MOSOP decided it would not be possible to secure any concessions from the federal government without international support.

Though he successfully propagated his message in Nigeria, his early attempts to garner worldwide attention showcased his naïveté with respect to global human rights activism. After penning the original Bill of Rights, Saro-Wiwa embarked on several tours abroad where he met with activist groups. During a tour of the United States in November 1990, he traveled to Denver, Colorado. There, he visited several environmental groups, including the Sierra Club and the Audubon Society. He later remarked in his prison diary, *A Month and a Day*, that these groups "showed what could be done by an environmental group to press demands on governments and companies."[5] He had previously struck up a friendship with Accra-born British author William Boyd, who encouraged him to contact human rights and environmental organizations, such as Greenpeace and Amnesty International. He recalled his conversations with these groups:

> It was to William that I turned whenever I hit a brick wall in my solicitation on behalf of the Ogoni. On his advice in 1991, I telephoned Greenpeace. "We don't work in Africa" was the chilling reply. When I called up Amnesty, I was asked "Is anyone dead? Is anyone in jail?" And when I replied in the negative, I was told nothing could be done. Was I upset? The Ogoni people were being killed, all right—but in an unconventional way. Amnesty was only interested in conventional killings. And as for Greenpeace, why would it not show concern for Africa? For Ogoni? It did seem that the Ogoni were destined for extinction.[6]

When Saro-Wiwa returned to Nigeria, he resolved to force the Ogoni cause on a global community that had long ignored his people's plight. He formulated his plan of action thus: "I sorted out in the back of my mind the two facets in the case: the complete devastation of the environment by the oil companies . . . and second: the political marginalization and economic strangulation of the Ogoni. . . . And I began to cast about for ways of confronting both institutions."[7] The main problem was how to connect the two in a way that mobilized not only the Ogoni but also the global community.

A year after the original Ogoni Bill of Rights, the Ogoni leadership added an addendum that included an appeal to the international community cementing the connection between Shell's actions and the environmental destruction of the Ogoni, which Saro-Wiwa termed genocide, a theme that transformed his activism, its global visibility, and the military government's harsh repression. Saro-Wiwa's blistering personal appeal at the end of the addendum lambasted the oil companies for their recklessness and negligence, the Nigerian government for stealing the fortunes that MOSOP and the broader Ogoni leadership believed to be their birthright, and brought the genocide contention to the forefront. Saro-Wiwa went even further, accusing Nigerian society as a whole of either willful collusion in this process or of selective blindness to the horrors inflicted on Nigerian minorities. In particular, he accused the Nigerian intelligentsia "who would ordinarily be expected to decry these actions, by their silence [lending] support to them."[8]

Saro-Wiwa ended his appeal with ten points, imploring the international community to put pressure on the Nigerian military government and the oil multinationals. All points address ways the international community could place pressure on the Nigerian government. The last two points state:

9. Prevail on European and American Governments to grant political refugee status to all Ogoni people seeking protection from the political persecution and *genocide* at the hands of the Federal Government of Nigeria.

10. Prevail on Shell and Chevron to pay compensation to the Ogoni People for ruining the Ogoni environment and the health of Ogoni men, women and children.

Though Saro-Wiwa had been developing the link between genocide and the Ogoni tragedy, the original Bill of Rights did not contain the word. It first appeared in point 9 of his personal addendum, and it signaled a marked change in his tactics. The importance of Saro-Wiwa's first use of the word *genocide* here cannot be understated. The word itself was coined in 1944 by Raphael Lemkin, in his work *Axis Rule in Occupied Europe*.[9] The term was later codified into international law by the United Nations Convention on the Prevention and Punishment of the Crime of Genocide (UNCP-PCG) of 1948, which defined genocide as

Any of the following acts committed with intent to destroy, in whole or in part, a national, ethnical, racial or religious group, as such:

Killing members of the group;

Causing serious bodily or mental harm to members of the group;

Deliberately inflicting on the group conditions of life calculated to bring about its physical destruction in whole or in part;

Imposing measures intended to prevent births within the group;

Forcibly transferring children of the group to another group.[10]

Saro-Wiwa knew well the successful propaganda war that Ojukwu's Biafra waged, calling the civil war against him a genocidal conflict. Saro-Wiwa had to find a way to internationalize his people's predicament in a way that would resonate globally and ensure effective mobilization. His goal was to build an international coalition that would pressure both the Nigerian government and the companies doing business with it. To this end, he connected the environmental catastrophe with the idea of genocide with the claim that the environmental damage was indeed "inflicting on the group conditions of life calculated to bring about its physical destruction in whole or in part," as the UNCPPCG stated. In the addendum to the Bill of Rights, Saro-Wiwa created the foundational document needed to publicize his people's difficulties worldwide.

Saro-Wiwa made sure the addendums included a provision designating MOSOP the sole authority to petition "to the United Nations Commission on Human Rights, the Commonwealth Secretariat, the African Commission on Human and Peoples rights, the European Community and all international bodies which have a role to play in the preservation of our nationality."[11] This provision made Saro-Wiwa the international mouthpiece for the Ogoni.

Utilizing his media contacts and friends in the literary community, Saro-Wiwa traveled to Geneva in the summer of 1992 to participate in the United Nations Working Group on Indigenous Populations (UNWGIP). Saro-Wiwa had worked with the Unrepresented Nations and Peoples Organization (UNPO) and through his EMIROAF organization was able to secure legitimacy for MOSOP within the UNPO. That October, British broadcaster Channel Four aired a documentary series titled *The Heat of the Moment*, which highlighted the impact of petroleum extraction on the Niger Delta and the Ogoni. Unlike his earlier attempts to engage Greenpeace and Amnesty International, these actions garnered the attention of some small but vocal environmental organizations, such as Earth First! and the London Rainforest Network. Saro-Wiwa had finally garnered a global audience who listened to his demands.

His exploits abroad were well publicized in Nigeria and led to a quick mobilization of the Ogoni but also drew increased attention from the country's security forces. To continue the mobilization in Nigeria, he published *Genocide in Nigeria: The Ogoni Tragedy,* a short pamphlet-style book chronicling the plight of the Ogoni in Nigeria and highlighting their suffering at the hands of colonial and Nigerian authorities, as well as Ogoni loyalty to Nigeria despite their travails. The book's goal was to galvanize support for MOSOP among the Ogoni and to emphasize the movement's nonviolent bona fides. Most important, *Genocide in Nigeria,* as the name stated, was his first forceful attempt at linking environmental calamity to the political and economic marginalization that the Ogoni suffered.

*Genocide in Nigeria* also detailed the collusion between the state and the multinational oil companies wreaking havoc in the Niger Delta. Saro-Wiwa chronicled the devastation beginning with the 1970 Bomu blowout and spill. Shell's actions, he argued, destroyed the Ogoni people, because the environmental destruction "has destroyed ALL wildlife, and plant life, poisoned the atmosphere and therefore the inhabitants in the surrounding areas and made the residents half-deaf and prone to respiratory disease."[12] The gas flaring, oil spills, and other disasters associated with the oil industry destroyed the environment so completely that Saro-Wiwa could only end his discussion with the following lament:

> Where are the antelopes, the squirrels, the sacred
> tortoises, the snails, the lions and tigers which
> roamed this land? Where are the crabs, periwinkles,
> mudskippers, cockles, shrimps and all which found
> sanctuary in mudbanks, under the protective roots of
> mangrove trees?

I hear in my heart the howls of death in the polluted
air of my beloved homeland; I sing a dirge for my
children, my compatriots and their progeny.[13]

Naturally, Saro-Wiwa could not hold Shell, Chevron, and the other oil companies solely responsible for the destruction. He lambasted the structure of power in Nigeria that placed the interests of the Igbo, Yoruba, and Hausa-Fulani, which Saro-Wiwa called the majority groups, above both minority rights and national unity. Coupled with the crippling corruption and theft from government coffers, Nigeria's political structure ensured that the Ogoni, and most of the ethnic groups located in the oil-producing areas, would continue to be marginalized. "Nothing works in Nigeria," Saro-Wiwa stated, "because rulers and ruled owe loyalty, not to the country, but to their ethnic groups."[14] For Saro-Wiwa, the utility of the Nigerian state and its mechanisms was judged by the ability to return rewards to the ethnic groups that controlled a particular state apparatus. Saro-Wiwa reminded his readers that the National Bank of Nigeria doled out money to the tune of NGN 1 billion in the form of unsecured loans "by its mainly Yoruba directors and clients," forcing it to declare bankruptcy in 1992.[15] Oil revenue gave the ethnic majority–controlled government an inexhaustible source of income without the burden of dealing with the disastrous consequences that the extraction of oil was having on the environment in the Niger Delta because the people who lived there had so little influence. The complicity between the oil companies and the government was "the nail in the Ogoni coffin," the title of one of the chapters in *Genocide in Nigeria.*

Saro-Wiwa had little choice but to resort to a direct confrontation against the government. He had previously tried to work from within the system to enact reforms, but his attempts had been futile, and he had witnessed an increase in the repression of the Ogoni. When Nigeria's first brief return to civilian rule ended on New Year's Eve in 1983, in a coup that ousted President Shehu Shagari following a rigged election, the coup's leader, Muhammadu Buhari, and his successors Ibrahim Badamasi Babangida and Sani Abacha further added a level of military repression unheard of in previous Nigerian regimes.

Both Buhari and Babangida combined repression with attempts to create a new, "disciplined society," many aspects of which became known as Buharism. Part of this campaign was a vigorous attempt to prosecute corrupt government officials from Shagari's government. In one instance, Buhari's government attempted to kidnap Shagari's minister of transportation, Umaru Dikko, who was accused of embezzling up to USD 1 billion. Dikko, who had fled to London after the 1983 coup, was tracked down by Israel's Mossad and Nigerian agents, who kidnapped and drugged him with the aid of an Israeli anesthesiologist recruited for the task. They then placed the drugged Dikko in a diplomatic mail crate on July 5, 1984. However, the mail crate did not include the proper documentation to prohibit search on diplomatic grounds, and Dikko was discovered in the mail, along with the Israeli doctor.[16]

At home, Saro-Wiwa became a part of the new military government's attempts to forge a nationalist identity for Nigeria. Shortly after the coup, Buhari began a plan, which he called the War Against Indiscipline (WAI). The plan was a combination of xenophobia and state-sponsored civic activism, including the monthly sanitation cleanup known colloquially as the "environmental." These anticorruption measures gave the state security apparatus considerable leeway in enforcement.[17] The civic activism also included mass destruction of buildings deemed illegal and a mass deportation of migrant workers from neighboring countries. The deportations led to a cottage industry of hastily constructed cheap plastic bags that Nigerians mockingly referred to as "Ghana Must Go" bags because of the many Ghanaians expelled from the country who used them to pack their belongings.[18] *Basi and Company,* which began its run on Nigerian television in 1985, contained many themes in line with those promoted by Buharism.

When a coup led by Babangida ousted Buhari in 1985, Babangida promised a quick return to civilian rule, but he continued many of Buhari's social-engineering projects. Many of Babangida's projects were aimed at influencing the elections, which he first scheduled in 1990, but repeatedly delayed until he eventually held them on June 12, 1993. Babangida's government co-opted Saro-Wiwa into Babangida's election plans and in

1989 named him executive director of the new Directorate for Social Mobilization's enforcement arm, called the Mass Mobilization for Self-Reliance, Social Justice, and Economic Recovery (MAMSER). MAMSER's policies echoed Buhari's WAI program in many ways and sought to encourage political participation and a national communal spirit. Saro-Wiwa held this position for a year but resigned after learning that he would be allowed no real authority within the organization.[19]

Once Saro-Wiwa finished organizing the Ogoni into the various organizations constituting MOSOP, he prepared for the next stage of his confrontation with the government: mass mobilization. He chose 1993 as the year for this for two reasons. First, the long-delayed transition to civilian rule was expected to take place in that year, with Babangida first declaring it would occur on January 2, 1993, before delaying it once again until August 27. Saro-Wiwa, ever a student of the theatrical, organized his January 4 march to coincide with the aborted handover of power and to celebrate the United Nations declaration of 1993 as the International Year for the World's Indigenous Populations. Saro-Wiwa stated in his prison diary that the date was chosen because Babangida

> was expected to hand over power on 2 January. If he did so, we would be serving notice to the new administration that the Ogoni people would no longer accept exploitation and a slave status in

Nigeria. If Babangida failed to hand over, we would be confronting him directly and daring him to do his worst.[20]

In reality, Saro-Wiwa knew that the handover would be delayed. He did not begin the preparations for the march until his return from Geneva in the summer of 1992, after the elections had already been postponed. He did not finalize the date for the march until December 1992, when it became clear that the election would not be held until the following June. He was, however, successful in mobilizing the Ogoni

**Figure 6.1** Saro-Wiwa addressing the crowd at the march and rally on January 2, 1993. Drawing by Kazeem Oyetunde Ekeolu

people, as an estimated 300,000 people from all six of the Ogoni kingdoms, which accounted for roughly two-thirds of the total Ogoni population, participated in the march and rally. Saro-Wiwa recalled how amazed he was by the resilience of the Ogoni despite the nervous tension when Saro-Wiwa and the other protest organizers discovered that the military had positioned forces to surround the Ogoni homeland. Despite their fears, the event proceeded and was well covered in the media, with both Greenpeace, who had previously refused to work in Africa, and the Rainforest Action Group sending photographers to cover both the environmental degradation and the Ogoni protest.

Despite the peaceful protest, tension and anger were palpable from the beginning. Even before the rally started a group of Ogoni youth symbolically "conquered" the Bomu oil field, which Shell had abandoned in anticipation of the day's events. The day culminated in a massive rally at Bori, where Saro-Wiwa symbolically declared Shell persona non grata, urging the Ogoni to continue the struggle and imploring the massive crowd "to fight relentlessly for your rights. As our cause is just, and God being our helper, we shall emerge victoriously over the forces of greed, wickedness and obduracy."[21]

Although the events on January 4 ignited a popular movement, it also led to increased state repression against the Ogoni and Saro-Wiwa. A month after the march, Saro-Wiwa traveled to The Hague to participate in the UNPO meeting and hold meetings with Shell officials. When he returned in February, he was summoned with Garrick Leton and Chief Edward Kobani to the offices of the head of the State Security Services (SSS). Kobani would later be one of the four chiefs murdered in 1994, initiating the chain of events leading to Saro-Wiwa's execution. Peter Ndiokwu, head of the SSS, warned Saro-Wiwa and his colleagues regarding their actions, especially those abroad. Ndiokwu hinted at the troubles ahead for Saro-Wiwa, emphasizing that should he continue, he would undoubtedly face incarceration.

Tensions heightened almost immediately within MOSOP when a group of Ogoni elders sought to distance themselves from the organization's activities and ingratiate themselves with the Babangida government. At the urging of the Rivers State governor, Rufus Ada-George, a group of Ogoni chiefs, who had initially signed the Bill of Rights in 1990, issued a proclamation stating that the protest was a success. They then thanked the government for listening to the Ogoni demands and promised no more marches or protests. Saro-Wiwa and the MOSOP leadership quickly responded, issuing a statement denying that these chiefs spoke for MOSOP and reiterating that MOSOP alone was authorized by the Bill of Rights as the sole voice of the Ogoni and the only legitimate organization to speak on their behalf.

In the following months, Saro-Wiwa was a marked man. After the January protests, Shell began its cooperative campaign with the government to protect oil workers in Ogoniland and to undermine MOSOP's ability to represent Ogoni interests. Between March and April, Saro-Wiwa was arrested several times, his home and office ransacked to find evidence of some treasonous offense.

Shell and its contractors also regularly hired Nigerian military escorts to support their work, a practice they would admit years later.[22] On April 30, 1993, soldiers escorting pipeline workers working for Wilbros, who were building a second pipe on the Trans-Niger pipeline, arrived in the town of Biara. The pipeline had spilled there two years prior, and the work detail was met with protesters holding twigs as a symbol of nonviolence. The soldiers opened fire, injuring eleven protesters. The next day, thousands of protesters took to the streets in Biara and elsewhere, where more clashes erupted; at least one protester was killed, and the pipeline crews were forced to retreat. This event signaled the beginning of a violent repression campaign against the Ogoni coinciding with the 1993 presidential elections.

Preparations for the elections, originally scheduled for December 5, 1992, turned to chaos during the nomination process. No fewer than twenty-three candidates sought the nomination of one of the two artificial parties that Babangida created, the Social Democratic Party (SDP) and the National Republican Convention (NRC). In the end, the SDP nomination went to Shehu Yar'Adua, elder brother of Umaru Yar'Adua who would later serve as president from 2007 to 2010, and Adamu Ciroma, a former governor of the Central

Bank of Nigeria, won the NRC nomination. However, the losers in the primaries complained of voting irregularities and vote rigging. These complaints prompted Babangida to cancel the primary results and postpone the election to June 12, 1993. Further, the candidate field was reduced from twenty-three to two: Chief Moshood Kashimawo Olawale Abiola (nicknamed MKO), a Yoruba businessman and media tycoon who became the SDP nominee, and Bashir Tofa, a businessman from Kano, the NRC candidate.

Though the presidential election proceeded in an orderly fashion and was the fairest and most transparent in Nigerian history, Babangida annulled the result ten days after the election, invalidating Abiola's victory. Some political critics pointed out that both candidates were Muslim and that they both contested the election as evidence that Babangida sought to create an election that would be too close to call, allowing for the indefinite extension of military rule.[23] However, Abiola won convincingly with 58 percent of the vote, even winning Tofa's home state of Kano. Babangida argued that Abiola exploited ethnic tensions, and he claimed that there was widespread voter fraud and vote purchasing.

Saro-Wiwa decided to use the election as a referendum for MOSOP among the Ogoni. On June 2, he called a meeting of MOSOP, where he proposed a boycott of the elections. Although most of the MOSOP leadership supported the election boycott, several powerful members did not. Among those who did not support

121

the boycott were Leton, Kobani, and Albert Badey, all old-guard politicians who sought to be involved in the new political order. Saro-Wiwa's refusal to rescind the election boycott caused a schism within the MOSOP leadership, leading Leton and the others to announce that MOSOP had lifted the boycott on Saro-Wiwa's orders, without the latter's knowledge. The election, and the Ogoni response to it, became a central issue in the struggle for power among the Ogoni leadership.

Despite the dissenters' attempts, the boycott was very effective, adding to the turmoil within MOSOP. Members of MOSOP's youth organization, the National Youth Council of Ogoni People (NYCOP), actively enforced the boycott, with Saro-Wiwa himself admitting that NYCOP at times acted too enthusiastically. Saro-Wiwa's enemies accused him of orchestrating the violence, using NYCOP as his own paramilitary wing. Most NYCOP members were disenfranchised youth, some of them members of a semi-organized crime syndicate known in Nigeria as "Area Boys." These groups helped enforce the boycott, even going so far as to block ballot box transportation. One group even blockaded Kobani's home, forcing him to remain inside during the election.

Newspapers in Nigeria and abroad reported extensively on the boycott, raising MOSOP's profile and making their leader even more of a threat to a government hovering on the brink of collapse. Babangida's reaction to the election triggered a wave of violence, as groups opposed to the annulment organized to protest. In the south, where Abiola held sway, many pro-democracy organizations united to form the Campaign for Democracy (CD). In the north, government-funded "AstroTurf" organizations came into being to support Babangida, who declared a state of emergency in many parts of the country, including Ogoniland. The Babangida government enforced the Treason and Treasonous Felony Law passed after the Ogoni Bill of Rights. This law made any attempt to argue for ethnic autonomy equivalent to secession, and thus a treasonous offense. MOSOP's boycott of the election gave Babangida cause to arrest Saro-Wiwa, who was imprisoned for a month, where he wrote his incarceration diary *A Month and a Day.*

Saro-Wiwa's arrest and detention caused a global uproar and marked the turning point of the Ogoni struggle, as human and environmental rights groups from around the world rallied to his aid, putting more strain on an already embattled Babangida. Amnesty International declared Saro-Wiwa a prisoner of conscience. The UNWGIP, UNPO, Greenpeace, and the Association of Nigerian Authors all lobbied around the world for his case, and Saro-Wiwa was eventually released and the state ordered to compensate him. A shaken, but undeterred, Saro-Wiwa ended his prison memoir with a prophetic note, "The genocide of the Ogoni had taken on a new dimension. The manner of it I will narrate in my next book, if I live to tell the tale."[24]

Babangida's woes were not limited to the Ogoni. The uncertainty over the election outcome sparked fears of a new civil war and mass migrations, not seen in the country since 1966, as people returned to their ethnic homelands from all across the country. To ease fears, Babangida did step down at the assigned August 27 date, but handed power to a close ally, Ernest Shonekan, who headed an interim governing council (IGC). The IGC did not, as many expected, hand over power to Abiola. Rather, Shonekan attempted to entrench himself in power, raising the price of gasoline in the country fivefold. In November, the courts declared the IGC unconstitutional and sided with Abiola, ruling that only the winner of the election could wield authority, leading to a further crisis of legitimacy.

In the end, neither Abiola nor the IGC controlled the country. On November 17, 1993, General Sani Abacha ousted the IGC and declared himself head of state and commander of the armed forces. Abacha's reign, lasting until his death in 1998, proved to be the pinnacle of corruption and brutality in Nigeria, setting up a showdown with Saro-Wiwa that ended nearly two years later, on November 10, with Saro-Wiwa's execution.

# The Trials and
# Death of Saro-Wiwa

Ken Saro-Wiwa could not have chosen a more dangerous time to begin his mass movement. Although he directly confronted the Babangida regime in the run-up to the 1993 elections, the election result and the dictator's response to it created a crisis that led to Sani Abacha taking power in a coup later that year. Abacha's ruthlessness added a new dimension to the already corrupt regime, and Saro-Wiwa would feel the full force of Abacha's brutality. Abacha's rise to power in Nigeria signaled the beginning of a period unprecedented in Nigerian history. According to some estimates, Abacha pilfered up to GBP 6 billion from Nigerian government coffers, leading Transparency International to name him the fourth most corrupt head of government in the twentieth century after Suharto of Indonesia, Ferdinand Marcos of the Philippines, and Mobutu Sese Seko of Zaire.[1] In addition to the graft that became endemic at all levels of Nigeria's government, Abacha added a staggering level of state repression. None were more vulnerable to Abacha than those who, like Saro-Wiwa, aimed to challenge the oil industry, Nigeria's main source of income and the source of much of Abacha's stolen wealth.

By 1993, MOSOP had succeeded in bringing the Ogoni situation to global attention. Both the January 4 march and the June 12 boycott showed the Nigerian government that Saro-Wiwa could effectively mobilize the Ogoni. These events also exposed fissures in the Ogoni leadership between Saro-Wiwa and the elder political elites. Saro-Wiwa commanded the support of most of the Ogoni population, particularly the youth. The elder political elites were led by Kobani and Leton and supported by the Rivers State government and the oil companies, led by Shell. Leton felt that because Saro-Wiwa's activism had generated such publicity at home and abroad that it was time for a formal reconciliation with the Nigerian government, which would surely include concessions on the government's part. Saro-Wiwa supported continued action to bring the Ogoni cause to the forefront of Nigerian and global awareness. This disagreement began a power struggle between the two factions, culminating on May 21, 1994, with the murder of Kobani and three other Ogoni leaders. These murders gave the federal government the opportunity to destroy the Ogoni leadership and to execute Saro-Wiwa, thus removing the head of the populist movement that had been pestering them and jeopardizing their economic interests in the Niger Delta.

Once Saro-Wiwa announced the election boycott, the Nigerian military dictatorship, with Shell's alleged support, initiated a crackdown on the Ogoni, with the aim of resuming Shell's operations by whatever means necessary. The shots fired at eleven protesters on April 30, 1993, and the resulting riots, in which one was killed, discussed in chapter 6, marked the first of a series of government-orchestrated paramilitary actions. After the elections, the Babangida government intensified the campaign against the Ogoni. On July 9, and again at the beginning of August, hundreds of Ogoni were massacred, first with the attack on an Ogoni group returning from Cameroon along the Andoni River and weeks later with the razing of the village of Kaa, at the southern end of Ogoniland. Though the government blamed interethnic warfare between the Ogoni and Andoni for the massacres, eyewitness accounts disputed that assertion. The journalist Karl Maier, who arrived at Kaa a few days after the massacre, witnessed the remnants of the battle. Maier stated that the weaponry used, which included mortar and hand grenades, was indicative of a military operation. Eyewitnesses to the attack on Kaa and subsequent attacks told Maier that they were perpetrated by well-armed men in uniform. In a conversation with Maier, Claude Ake, one of the most renowned Nigerian political scientists, questioned the alleged Andoni motives. "The Andonis depended on the market at Kaa to sell their fish. What would be the purpose of destroying their own livelihood?"[2]

The Kaa massacre signaled a new violent government tactic against the Ogoni. Within months the Ogoni came under attack from practically all neighboring ethnic groups. In December, the Okrika attacked, and in April 1994, an Ndoki raid killed twenty people and destroyed eight villages. Publicly, the Nigerian government blamed the Ogoni for the violence, stating that the attacks were merely retribution for past transgressions. Lieutenant-Colonel Paul Okuntimo, head of the Rivers State internal security task force, began a reign of terror against the Ogoni, culminating in his masterminding the attacks that killed Kobani. In fact, Okuntimo exerted constant pressure on all aspects of Saro-Wiwa's trial for the murder of Kobani and the other chiefs, including beatings of defense counsel and members of Saro-Wiwa's family, making a fair trial virtually impossible.

Okuntimo told the Ogoni, "You killed the Andonis . . . so we came and chased you people. After the Andonis, you fought with the Ndokis. So they invited us to chase you people."[3] Privately, however, Okuntimo and the rest of the Nigerian high command in Delta State were more concerned about Shell's operations. Okuntimo allegedly sent a secret memo, dated just days before the chiefs' murders, in which he advocated "wasting operations during MOSOP and other gatherings," stating that Shell would not be able to resume drilling "unless ruthless military operations are undertaken for smooth economic activities to commence."[4] Okuntimo also advised that Shell would be responsible for the costs of these military operations. On one occasion, Okuntimo's orderly, a man named Boniface

Ejiogu, witnessed the lieutenant colonel and his soldiers loading seven large "Ghana Must Go" bags filled with cash from a Shell facility.[5]

Thus, when the four Ogoni chiefs were brutally murdered, the event was the outcome of complex power struggles both within MOSOP and between the Ogoni leadership and the Nigerian military regime; the military sought stability in the wake of the aborted election and two quick changes of power, culminating with the rise of Sani Abacha. Additionally, Shell concessions in the Ogoni territory were losing the company money, and the firm wished to resume its operations as quickly as possible.

Saro-Wiwa contested a lost election for a seat on a new constitutional conference, to be held on May 23, 1994. Kobani's group actively campaigned against him in their attempt to ensure that he would not get elected as the Ogoni representative. After Saro-Wiwa held several rallies on the May 20, Kobani feared Saro-Wiwa was organizing the National Youth Council of Ogoni People (NYCOP) in order to ensure an effective election boycott as he had the year before. The next day, Kobani contacted security forces in the area, notifying them where Saro-Wiwa's demonstrations would be held. The security forces intercepted Saro-Wiwa and refused to allow him to continue to the Gokana kingdom, forcing his return to Port Harcourt. Initial reports stated that Ogoni youth, angered by Saro-Wiwa's inability to attend the gatherings, descended on the palace of the

Gbenemene of Gokana, where Kobani was meeting with Albert Badey and the Orage brothers, Samuel and Theophilus, both former government officials and Gokana chiefs. All four were beaten to death by the mob. Charles Tambou, editor of Port Harcourt's *Sunray* newspaper, phoned Saro-Wiwa to inform him of the killings. Saro-Wiwa reportedly replied, "Oooooh! My God, they have finished me!"[6]

In 2010, new testimony appeared that contradicted the allegations of the initial account. This new account, taken from Ejiogu's deposition in a trial Saro-Wiwa's family brought against Shell, placed the blame squarely on the military and painted the killings as one of the "wasting operations." When a military investigator asked about the deaths of Kobani and the others, Okuntimo allegedly replied, "Maybe the boys [the soldiers on the scene] started getting crazy. That is all."[7] This testimony is consistent with Okuntimo's "wasting" memo, which stressed the need for brutality to suppress the Ogoni movement.

Nevertheless, the next day Dauda Musa Komo, the military governor of Rivers State, placed blame firmly on MOSOP's shoulders. "Ogoni is bleeding," Komo stated at a press conference that day, "not by federal troops, genocidal federal troops, as some of the papers carried some days back, but by irresponsible and reckless thuggery of the MOSOP element, which . . . must stop immediately."[8] By the time Komo made the statement, security forces had already arrested Saro-Wiwa, accusing him of ordering the killings.

The following months saw Okuntimo's forces rampage throughout Ogoniland, with almost nightly attacks on Ogoni towns and villages. Human Rights Watch/Africa (HRW/A) reported that at least sixty towns were attacked. The group collected testimonies from both the perpetrators and the victims. One soldier who participated in a raid on the village of Kpor stated, "We were shooting as we drove in. Women were screaming and crying. The young men ran. We shot at them. They told us to capture the place. We went into the bush and saw some corpses. I was firing randomly. I shot three people that day. I aimed at them when they ran and shot them down."[9] One twenty-year-old victim of an assault on Bori, Saro-Wiwa's home, recalled his chilling experience:

> I felt the bullet hit me in the leg. The soldier who fired was standing only three yards away. Then many shots were fired, hitting the ground near me. I pretended that I was dead. The commander called to another soldier, who cocked his gun, pointed, and fired at the guy lying down nearest to me. I saw that he was bleeding. There was blood in a pool near his body. Then the commander ordered five soldiers to stay with us and guard the trucks. The five had too many people to watch. Slowly, I began to drag myself off the road, towards the bush. It was dark and raining, and after I had crawled a few yards, they couldn't see me very well. I rolled away and hid behind some trees.[10]

Okuntimo hoped the murders, executions, rapes, looting, and destruction of entire villages would encourage the Ogoni leadership to negotiate a settlement. In fact, he coupled the brutality with meetings with the Ogoni leadership in twenty-seven communities where he went about "addressing rallies, addressing people, asking them to have a change of heart."[11] However, at one of the meetings, he boasted about having learned 204 ways to kill a person, adding that he would welcome the opportunity to demonstrate all of them to the Ogoni.[12]

The Abacha regime's brutality was not limited only to the Ogoni or to Saro-Wiwa. Unlike Babangida, Abacha tolerated no political opposition and reacted brutally to suppress any challenge to his sole authority over the country. Abiola, the winner of the 1993 elections, was arrested in the summer of 1994 after declaring himself the rightful leader of Nigeria, effectively ratifying the results of the June 12 election. Abacha later agreed to a conditional release for Abiola, provided he renounce any claims to have won the election, a demand Abiola refused. He died in prison in 1998, under suspicious circumstances, on the day he was to be released. Similarly, Shehu Yar'Adua was convicted of treason in 1995 for demanding a return to civilian rule. He too died in prison, in 1997. However, Saro-Wiwa was singled out for special consideration because of his success in mobilizing support for the Ogoni cause abroad and especially for the pressure his efforts placed on Shell, which regarded him as a menace and monitored his activities closely.

Fifteen other Ogoni leaders were arrested along with Saro-Wiwa. They were held from May until November without charge and with no access to their attorneys. In the meantime, Abacha created a new tribunal, called the Civil Disturbances Special Tribunal (CDST) and designed it to ensure a guilty verdict. The CDST consisted of two judges and a military officer, and the accused were given no right to appeal the court's verdict, even in the case of the death penalty, which was expressly in the tribunal's mandate. Practically every aspect of the tribunal contravened both Nigerian and international codes of the judiciary, as set forth by the International Covenant on Civil and Political Rights (ICCPR), which Nigeria had ratified. However, even the chief prosecutor, Philip Umeadi, scoffed at the legal aspects of the case, stating that Nigeria was a "primitive society" and could not be held to the same standards as the developed world.[13]

By the time Saro-Wiwa and his colleagues were officially charged, on January 28, 1995, the court's proceedings were so obviously flawed that it was clear that the group would not be tried fairly. The official charge was incitement to murder. When Saro-Wiwa and the others gained access to their attorneys, it was only in the presence of Okuntimo, who created an atmosphere of intimidation that helped guarantee the trial's continued opacity.

Because the court was structured in a way to pervert justice, the guilty verdict and sentence seemed preordained. Ibrahim Auta, the tribunal chairman, ruled that this special tribunal need not heed the ordinary Nigerian laws governing murder; he said that it was enough to show that Saro-Wiwa and his codefendants incited

Figure 7.1 Saro-Wiwa and his codefendants in the courtroom in Port Harcourt, June 1995. Drawing by Kazeem Oyetunde Ekeolu

violence and caused the civil disturbance ending in the murders of the four chiefs. The flagrant violations of due process caused Saro-Wiwa's defense team to resign in protest in June 1995.

Even before the trial started, several problems arose that made it clear the verdict was premeditated. Some of the prosecution's witnesses admitted to being bribed for their testimony. One such witness, Charles Danwi, a struggling musician, testified that Alhaji Mohammed Kobani (brother of Edward Kobani) promised him a house, a job with the Gokana local government, and NGN 30,000. Other witnesses were also less than credible and presumably selected for their personal animosity toward Saro-Wiwa. One, Celestine Meabe, had been accused of using the NYCOP offices in the Gokana kingdom as a front for vigilante activities. Saro-Wiwa ordered him to disband his group. When he refused, he was ejected from NYCOP and MOSOP. In exchange for his perjured testimony, Meabe was given the same benefits as Danwi.

Accompanying these flagrant violations of due process, the military dictatorship employed other methods to ensure a guilty verdict. Anyone wishing to enter the court building first needed accreditation, which was rarely given. In at least one instance, Saro-Wiwa's own defense lawyers were denied entry to the building, and when they protested, the police beat one member of the team, human rights lawyer Femi Falana. The ever-present Okuntimo presided over the beating of Saro-Wiwa's aging mother outside the courtroom in Port Harcourt. Saro-Wiwa's wife and sister-in-law were also beaten. When the family protested, Okuntimo arrested two of Saro-Wiwa's half brothers.

Okuntimo's presence loomed in all aspects of the case against Saro-Wiwa and the other defendants. Michael Birnbaum, a British attorney and observer at the trial, penned a report in July 1995 highlighting the many irregularities of the proceedings. In one instance on July 26, 1994, two Nigerian attorneys, Oronto Douglas and Uche Onyeagocha, along with British environmentalist Nicholas Ashton-Jones arrived at Bori Military camp to see Saro-Wiwa. Saro-Wiwa was not at the camp, but the guard allowed the group to meet with Ledum Mitee. Okuntimo later arrived at the camp. Incensed, he drew his pistol, grabbed their police escort by the neck and kicked him in the groin, yelling, "What are these people doing here, who is this white man and these two men? Why can't you people take common instruction? You beasts, why did you allow them?"[14] Douglas, in an article published in the May 1994 issue of *Liberty,* recalled the ordeal of their ensuing three-day incarceration. Okuntimo left the three in the care of the regimental sergeant major (RSM):

> [The RSM] ordered that the cell be opened, took us to a room and ordered the soldiers to remove our shoes and that we be given "one hundred strokes of the cane, each." The cane was an electric cable. They flogged us mercilessly, brutally. No part of our bodies was spared. Uche's face was smashed with a soldier's boot. Nick's back and buttocks disfigured.[15]

Ashton-Jones later recalled that the soldiers administering the punishment were "as afraid of Major Okuntimo as we were," with one of them having Okuntimo's pistol "pushed down his throat . . . so we did not feel anything bad about him."[16] Okuntimo later returned, forced the visitors into a jeep at gunpoint and drove them away, detaining them for three days. In the jeep, Okuntimo said that Saro-Wiwa had been taken to a different location, shackled and denied food. He later said that he would "sanitize" Ogoniland to make it safe for Shell's operations. After three days of beatings, the trio were finally released, only after convincing Okuntimo that they too were working for Shell's best interests.

Birnbaum also raised concerns about Okuntimo's influence over the proceedings of the trial itself. In one instance, on March 27, 1995, Birnbaum met in private with the prosecution. At some point during the meeting, after what Birnbaum called "a very frank and helpful discussion," Okuntimo arrived uninvited and sat down to participate. No one present asked him to leave. In fact, Okuntimo would occasionally interject his opinions regarding the case. The defense attorneys later confided to Birnbaum that they suspected Okuntimo was in charge of security at the proceedings, including the many armed guards in the courtroom, and that he had direct and unfettered access to the tribunal itself. Birnbaum concluded that "[Okuntimo's] uninvited presence at my meeting with prosecuting counsel must give rise to fears that their independence has been compromised."[17]

Birnbaum's account chronicled not only Okuntimo's brutality and alleged influence over the court, but also irregularities in the proceedings themselves. In addition to obvious instances of witness tampering and bribery, the court failed to adhere to the established standards of evidence and admitted testimony that was clearly hearsay, rumor, and opinion. One of the accused, Garrick Leton, a former MOSOP president, turned on Saro-Wiwa, calling him a habitual liar and "a person who uses the travails of his people to achieve his selfish desires and ambitions . . . a person who in this situation cannot escape complicity in the murder of the four prominent Ogoni leaders."[18] Birnbaum recalled that this testimony was admitted into evidence, even though it in no way implicated Saro-Wiwa in any crime and was clearly hearsay. There was very little substantial evidence to convict Saro-Wiwa of any complicity in the killings, except for some conflicting testimonies that he may have addressed the crowd when he was stopped on the day of the killings, with the most damning evidence coming from bribed witnesses. As previously mentioned, Auta felt the trial did not need to adhere to the rules regarding guilt or innocence that were standard in the Nigerian civilian courts. All the court had to prove was that Saro-Wiwa's failure to appear at the rally inflamed the participants and transformed them into a lynch mob. Birnbaum remarked, "This guilt-by-association argument was complemented by an almost complete reversal of the burden of proof. These dishonest rulings could only have been given by a tribunal seeking to achieve a preordained decision."[19] Not only did Leton's evidence call into question the tribunal's integrity and impartiality, but it also exposed the acrimony within the Ogoni and MOSOP leadership, as the various leaders distanced themselves from Saro-Wiwa in an effort to save their own lives.

On April 2, 1995, less than a week after the meeting at which Okuntimo arrived unannounced, Birnbaum sent a letter to both the defense and the prosecution requesting all publicly available information relating to the murders of Kobani and the other leaders. He never heard from the prosecutors. A newspaper article quoted Umeadi describing Birnbaum and the other international observers as "a bunch of loafers looking for something to do," and saying further that their sole reason for attending the trial was to ascertain "whether we behave or not as our colonial masters." Birnbaum concluded, "I do not expect to receive any further co-operation from the prosecution."[20] The prosecution's sudden change in demeanor toward Birnbaum was indicative of Okuntimo's influence over the proceedings.

Various human rights organizations, such as the Human Rights Watch/Africa created an international uproar, with almost universal condemnation of the Nigerian government and Shell, which these organizations viewed as an active accomplice. Shell executives never denied paying for police protection, especially mobile police (MOPOL) protection, but, according to HRW/A, stated that

> Nigerian law requires them to contact the military administrator of Rivers State, the Rivers State police commissioner, the Department of Petroleum Resources, and Shell's joint venture partners, including the Nigerian National Petroleum Corporation. Shell executives maintained that the company's communications with the Rivers State military authorities are otherwise minimal.

Adding that:

> The company is required by law to [contact the authorities] when operations are threatened with

disruption. In this situation, a Shell company has no choice but to comply with the laws of the country, be it Nigeria or any other. We do not accept, however, that this makes [Shell] responsible for the actions the authorities then take. Nor does it mean that we condone such actions. . . . We categorically reject violence as a means of settling disputes.[21]

Shell's attitude did little to deflect criticism, given the carnage the Nigerian forces were committing in Ogoniland and the allegations of bribery. Saro-Wiwa's brother Owens pleaded with David Anderson, the Nigerian-born head of Shell's Nigerian operations, to intervene to stop the violence and trial. Anderson agreed to intervene, but only if MOSOP released a statement that no environmental damage had been done and that MOSOP end its campaign against Shell, terms to which Owens could not agree.[22]

Birnbaum later published a second account of the court proceedings, a report for *The Times*, following Saro-Wiwa's execution. In both accounts he criticized the trial's jurisprudence, mentioning that the trial lacked any semblance of due process. He concluded:

The judgment of the Tribunal is not merely wrong, illogical or perverse. It is downright dishonest. The Tribunal consistently advanced arguments which no experienced lawyer could possibly believe to be logical or just. I believe that the Tribunal first decided on its verdicts and then sought for arguments to justify them. No barrel was too deep to be scraped.[23]

Others shared Birnbaum's assessment; Saro-Wiwa's eldest son claimed he had premonitions that the judgment would be harsh, but thought international pressure would force Abacha to commute any death sentence, and that at worst, Saro-Wiwa would join Abiola and Obasanjo in prison. Very few believed that Abacha would go through with the executions for several reasons. First, Abacha and Saro-Wiwa knew each other very well, having been neighbors in Port Harcourt. Ken Wiwa recalled playing with Abacha's children as a child. Second, few thought that Abacha would risk the potential international backlash that would result from executing the nine defendants after such a kangaroo court proceeding.

The guilty verdicts were handed down on October 31, 1995, for Saro-Wiwa and eight of his codefendants: Saturday Dobee, Nordu Eawo, Daniel Gbooko, Paul Levera, Felix Nuate, Baribor Bera, Barinem Kiobel, and John Kpuinen, collectively called "The Ogoni Nine." The others were acquitted in what Birnbaum called "cosmetic acquittals."[24] Abacha confirmed the death sentences on November 8.

Saro-Wiwa wrote a statement but was denied permission to it read at his sentencing. The statement, an indictment of the court proceedings and the state of Nigeria as a whole, read in part:

> We all stand on trial, my lord, for by our actions
> we have denigrated our Country and jeopardized
> the future of our children. As we subscribe to the

sub-normal and accept double standards, as we lie and cheat openly, as we protect injustice and oppression, we empty our classrooms, denigrate our hospitals, fill our stomachs with hunger and elect to make ourselves the slaves of those who ascribe to higher standards, pursue the truth, and honour justice, freedom, and hard work. I predict that the scene here will be played and replayed by generations yet unborn. Some have already cast themselves in the role of villains, some are tragic victims, some still have a chance to redeem themselves. The choice is for each individual.[25]

Wole Soyinka, the Nobel laureate, then in exile, traveled to New Zealand along with Ken Wiwa on November 9 to persuade the Commonwealth heads of government to pressure Abacha to commute the death sentences. Wiwa had hoped to meet with Nelson Mandela to convince the South African president to take a firm stance against Abacha. However, Soyinka recalled only the despair he felt when he was met with disbelief that Abacha would go through with the execution, which Abacha had confirmed the previous day.

The day after Abacha confirmed the sentences, as Ken Wiwa met with the Commonwealth heads to try to save his father's life, nine coffins were brought to Port Harcourt prison. However, because the prison had not hosted an execution since Nigeria's independence, executioners had to be flown in from Northern Nigeria. The executions took place the following day, November 10, 1995. Saro-Wiwa and his fellow victims were transported from the military base where they had been held and reportedly did not know that they were to be executed until they were brought to the gallows.

Though no official account of the execution exists, several prisoners claimed to have witnessed the execution. Three witnesses were interviewed by *Africa Today*, which published an account of the execution, stating that Saro-Wiwa was the first to be brought to the gallows. He asked to see his wife one last time, but the guards refused his request. As they led him to the gallows, he shouted, "You can only kill the messengers, you cannot kill the message." They placed the noose around his neck, but the gallows malfunctioned, and he was removed in obvious distress. After some repairs, he was brought back in to be hanged, but again the gallows malfunctioned and he was taken from them, replaced with Kpunien. This time, the gallows functioned properly and the rest of the condemned were hanged, with Saro-Wiwa being the last to die. One of the prisoners stated that the execution was filmed, but no video ever surfaced, meaning there is still much uncertainty about the details of the execution. However, all accounts claim it took several tries to execute Saro-Wiwa, with some speculating that he was gifted with powers that prevented his execution.[26]

The heads of government suspended Nigeria from the Commonwealth on November 11, the day after the execution. European nations and the United States imposed some sanctions on Abacha's regime, including travel bans for military and political elites, but stopped short of approving an oil embargo, the one threat that would have crippled the Nigerian government. Mandela also depended on Shell's investment in South Africa, and as such could not afford to alienate the company.

The executions marked the beginning of a new chapter in Nigeria's repression of the Ogoni. By the end of 1995, most MOSOP leaders were either killed, jailed, forced underground, or exiled. Abroad, Saro-Wiwa became a symbol of the brutality of the Abacha regime, with many organizations using the execution as a rallying cry, much to the chagrin of many in the MOSOP leadership and those close to Saro-Wiwa. Saro-Wiwa's son Ken lamented that organizations that previously denied requests to assist MOSOP "were now falling over themselves to write proposals and get funding for projects to ensure that 'Ken Saro-Wiwa's death was not in vain.'"[27] Saro-Wiwa's death did little to heal the breaks within the Ogoni leadership, as MOSOP splintered into various autonomous groups, with Owens Wiwa based in Toronto and Ledum Mitee, who was also on trial with Saro-Wiwa, but acquitted, working at MOSOP's UK office in London.

The different factions within MOSOP had decidedly different agendas and worked in a morass of conflicting outside interests. Saro-Wiwa's execution increased the profile of the Ogoni movement and connected it with the various pro-democracy movements working to free Abiola, Yar'Adua, and Obasanjo and restore civilian rule in the country. However, the conflicts and power struggles within MOSOP thwarted any ability to reorganize the movement in the wake of Saro-Wiwa's death. Clifford Bob, a scholar of political movements and media use, blamed internal factions in MOSOP for fostering confusion through careless use of the internet, among other reasons. The internal squabbles eroded international support for MOSOP, causing global organizations to either minimize their operations in support of the Ogoni or to broaden their programs to include other Niger Delta minorities. The public battles surrounding almost every aspect of MOSOP's activities came to a high-profile head when, in 2000, the Nigerian government consented to the reburial of the Ogoni Nine. Saro-Wiwa's family wished that the victims would be separated, to obey Saro-Wiwa's last wishes, and invited a pathologist to identify the remains. However, others in the Ogoni leadership wanted to use the reburial to reinvigorate the movement and called for the group to be reburied together. In the end, Saro-Wiwa was buried in his own grave, while the other members of the Ogoni Nine were reburied together not far away.[28]

The aftermath of Saro-Wiwa's execution briefly gave the Ogoni movement more exposure than it had had previously, but the internal discord that existed during Saro-Wiwa's lifetime became more pronounced after his death. The strife dampened Saro-Wiwa's legacy, but the manner of his life and death has left several indelible marks and created a legacy that continues to reverberate decades after his execution.

# The Many Legacies of Ken Saro-Wiwa

Although Ken Saro-Wiwa's life ended prematurely on that fateful morning of November 10, 1995, he left an indelible mark on the life of Nigeria. His love of language, literature, and politics and his engagement with global human rights and environmental protection activism are legacies as multifaceted as the man himself. Virtually everyone with whom he connected during his extremely productive life was affected by these legacies, including his supporters in global movements for minorities' rights, his friends and enemies in Nigerian politics, and his peers in the literary world. However, of all the people who must resolve what Ken Saro-Wiwa meant, none are more important than his family, especially his children. His son, also named Kenule, stated in an interview on Canadian television that "he achieved in one lifetime what would take six or seven men to achieve."[1]

Had he never become involved in the struggle against Shell and the environmental destruction of the Niger Delta, Saro-Wiwa would still have a solid legacy in the literary world. He had a unique ability to engage his worldwide audience with his works at multiple levels. Although he owed his commercial success to projects like *Basi and Company,* one of the most popular television programs in Nigerian history, he transitioned to the highbrow literary world with an uncanny ease that eludes most writers who attempt it. Kehinde Ayoola of Obafemi Awolowo University called Saro-Wiwa the Nigerian Mark Twain.[2] Ayoola was referring to Saro-Wiwa's use of a local vernacular to create an entirely unique subset of English literature, but the comparison is apt in other respects as well. Both Saro-Wiwa and Twain were astute political commentators and both were business entrepreneurs, though Saro-Wiwa was more successful in this aspect than Twain.

Because of his early successes in the business world, Saro-Wiwa was able to send his wife and children to England in 1978. As a result, he spent most of the remainder of his life away from them. Aside from his few visits to England and the summers the family spent in Nigeria, he had little time together with his children. In fact, his daughter Noo recalled her shock when she discovered, at age fourteen, that her father had fathered a second family in Nigeria, keeping their existence hidden from her. When he finally revealed this to them, he enlisted his brother to break the news, rather than tell them himself. Noo and Ken have both written about their father's legacy and their struggle to come to terms with a father of global renown who was largely absent from their lives.

Kenule and Noo each take a very different approach to their larger-than-life yet largely neglectful father. His oldest son Kenule was entitled to use the Saro (meaning "firstborn") designation in his name, yet chose to go by the name Ken Wiwa, largely because of the his desire to differentiate his identity from his father's. At the beginning of his book *In the Shadow of a Saint*, he writes: "My father. Where does he end and where do I begin?"[3] Kenule scrutinized much of his professional and personal life in comparison with his father's life; even his marriage to an English woman and not to an Ogoni was subject to self-criticism in comparison with his father's legacy.

Unlike Kenule, Noo embraces the conflict that her father created in their identity. She explores her own relationship with Nigeria, and by extension with her father. Using the sharp wit that characterizes her father's writing, her travel memoir, *Looking for Transwonderland,* is at times deadly serious when discussing the problems that pervade the country of her birth and at other times hilarious when looking at Nigeria's culture and customs from the point of view of a person who is both native and expatriate. At the beginning of the book, she discusses her chagrin at having to spend her childhood summers in Port Harcourt instead of going on luxury vacations like her classmates in the United Kingdom. She expounds on the privations that she suffered as a young British girl spending time in a country with no running water, no electricity, and, above all, no television.

When, in 2006, she decided to return to Nigeria, she did so to reconcile herself with the meaning of being a Nigerian who lived most of her life as an expatriate. In one anecdote, she traveled to the southeastern city of Calabar to visit the much-vaunted Tinapa retail center. After seeing the advertisements on CNN and other global media outlets, she expected a teeming consumer heaven. Instead, after forgoing a meal in the expectation of a Western-style food court or restaurant, she arrived at a tenantless development. After spending hours searching for anything resembling a restaurant, and being accosted by security guards who demanded to know why she had come, she found a man who explained the reasoning behind Tinapa. He claimed it was a corruption scam initiated by Cross Rivers State governor Donald Duke. Tinapa was, as Noo explained, "[Duke's] Big White Elephant, an excuse to build a project and collect kickbacks." After another hour, she finally found a motorcycle taxi, popularly called an "okada." Famished, she could only tell the driver to take her to Mr. Biggs, a Nigerian fast food chain.[4]

Both Noo and Kenule came to terms with having a very public father. Though Saro-Wiwa was uncommonly accomplished in all his endeavors, he paid a price for his success by alienating his children, who were left on their own to reconcile their personal issues with their father with the legacy of the man who was intricately linked with the country he loved. For Kenule Jr. and Noo, the public figure and the private father became all the more difficult to separate because the former robbed the children of the latter.

Perhaps Saro-Wiwa's most influential legacy is the one he left in social, community, and international activism. Saro-Wiwa's linking of environmental degradation to genocide expanded the definition of genocide in worldwide popular opinion. This created a new avenue of redress for oppressed peoples all over the world. Since Saro-Wiwa, genocide encompasses more than the direct physical extermination of an ethnic, racial, or religious group; it can include many other things, such as forced cultural assimilation, religious persecution, and the destruction of language.

Saro-Wiwa, acutely aware of the power of language, and of the word *genocide* in particular, articulated grievances in a new way, driving global activists to confront offending states and forcing a reckoning with any entity, public or private, that collaborated in perpetrating genocide. Thus, Saro-Wiwa not only expanded the definition of genocide in public opinion, if not in international law, he altered the perspective of the global community in a way that directly confronted governments, nongovernmental organizations, and corporations to seek justice for the aggrieved parties.

Even during Saro-Wiwa's lifetime, other ethnic groups in the Delta, witnessing the effectiveness of his mass mobilization, mimicked his tactics, even taking on identical organization names. The Ijo, who had long suffered in region's power struggles, created an organization named the Movement for the Survival of the Ijo Ethnic Nationality (MOSIEN) in the early 1990s. The Ijo, particularly in the area surrounding the oil center of Warri, were systematically marginalized in favor of another group, the Itsekiri, who controlled the local government areas in and around the city. The Ijo complained for decades about their marginalization in the region, echoing Saro-Wiwa's concerns about indigenous imperialism. Further to the west, other Ijo clans held more political power. In response to the Ijo's organizing, the Itsekiri created a mass mobilization movement of their own, the Movement for the Survival of the Itsekiri Ethnic Nationality, sharing the same acronym MOSIEN.

Like the Ogoni, the Ijo were also left impoverished by the misallocation of oil funds and the environmental degradation accompanying petroleum development in the Delta. By the mid-1980s, this economic neglect and political marginalization led to massive unemployment among Ijo youths, who blamed the elders for poor leadership in obtaining employment allocations with the oil companies and civil service. Many of the unemployed youth began arming themselves, forming militias to combat their marginalization, with some calling themselves the Egbesu Boys of Africa, after Egbesu, the Ijo god of war. Others named themselves the Niger Delta Volunteer Force (NDVF), inspired by the Adaka Boro revolt of 1966. By the 1990s, these groups obtained significant arms, including many smuggled weapons sold by Nigerian army officers returning from peacekeeping missions in Liberia and Sierra Leone.

In 2001 the NDVF changed its name to Federated Niger Delta Ijaw Communities (FNDIC). Under both incarnations, the group engaged in violent tactics as well as a savvy media campaign inspired by that of MOSOP. The dual approach seemed to work. By 2003, the oil companies, led by Chevron, the major concessionary in Warri, dealt directly with FNDIC leaders, offering their leaders contracts and scholarships to attend university abroad. Delta State Governor James Ibori, who in 2012 was sentenced to twelve years in British prison for fraud and money laundering, appointed FNDIC leaders to prominent positions in Warri local government. For a time it seemed that the Delta State governor, along with the oil companies, had successfully co-opted the major Ijo organizations and had driven a wedge between their leaders in much the same way that this had happened with MOSOP.

In December 2005, the NDVF transformed itself into the Movement for the Emancipation of the Niger Delta (MEND). Unlike the FNDIC, MEND refused to negotiate directly with Nigerian leadership and embarked on a systematic assault against the oil companies. In January 2006, the group attacked a Shell installation, kidnapping four expatriate workers. In other attacks, the group killed fourteen Nigerian soldiers in and around Warri that same month. In the following years, kidnappings of oil workers and other expatriates in Nigeria increased, along with attacks on oil installations, pipelines, and government facilities. Because MEND refused to deal directly with the oil companies or the government, various groups, such as FNDIC were employed as mediators.

MEND attacks continued unabated for several years. In 2009, President Umaru Yar'Adua proposed an amnesty for MEND militants, with plans to integrate the recipients into the workforce. By the end of the amnesty, over 15,000 operatives accepted the terms, handing in thousands of weapons, including eighteen gunboats. Despite the amnesty program, the Ijo region, like much of Ogoni, continues to suffer the same iniquities that led to MEND's emergence, namely environmental degradation and economic marginalization.

Saro-Wiwa's activism saw much success even during his lifetime, but it was after his death, and most likely because of it, that corporate entities were finally held to account for their offenses against the environment and collusion with the severe human rights abuses in the Niger Delta. Saro-Wiwa's family sued Shell in the American court system; the lawsuit accused Shell of collaborating with the Abacha regime in Saro-Wiwa's execution, as well as the torture of Saro-Wiwa's brother Owens. In 2009, Shell agreed to settle the lawsuit for USD 15.5 million while denying culpability for any wrongdoing.

The family's lawsuit was not the only one brought against Shell in the years since Saro-Wiwa's killing. Victims of Shell's oil activities have filed suits in the United States, the Netherlands, and Nigeria with varying degrees of success. Although a Nigerian court fined Shell in 2000, other suits have not been as successful in bringing the company to account. In one case filed in 2008, the environmentalist group Friends of the Earth filed a suit on behalf of four farmers who suffered from a series of spills that occurred between 2004 and 2007. Though the Dutch court in 2013 found Shell responsible and ordered the company to reimburse one of the farmers, it dismissed the cases against the other three.

In the United States, the Saro-Wiwa lawsuit was only possible due to an interpretation of the American Alien Tort Claims Act (ATCA). One of the oldest tort acts in US history, dating from 1789, the law states that US courts can enforce any treaty that the United States is a signatory to. In a 1980 case, a Paraguayan national, Dolly Filártiga, brought a suit against the chief of police of Asunción, the Paraguayan capital, claiming that he tortured and killed her son. This case set the precedent that victims of human rights abuses outside the United States can sue in American courts. This precedent held until 2013, when Barinem Kiobel and eleven other Ogoni leaders filed suit against Shell, accusing the company and its Nigerian subsidiaries of colluding with the Babangida and Abacha regimes in the human rights abuses against the Ogoni during the first half of the 1990s. In 2013, the US Supreme Court dismissed the lawsuit, claiming that the ATCA does not apply extraterritorially, but applies only to foreign nationals claiming abuses within the United States or US nationals committing crimes abroad or when dealing with enemies of mankind, *hostis humani generis.* This decision effectively ended lawsuits such as those brought by Saro-Wiwa's family and Kiobel. Other countries, such as the Netherlands and the United Kingdom, still allow such cases, as do international courts such as the International Court of Justice (ICJ). One such case is (as of the writing of this book in 2014) proceeding in UK courts involving two 2008 spills in Bodo, a town roughly 40 kilometers southwest of Port Harcourt. In 2015 Shell agreed to a settlement whereby it paid GBP 55 million. Of the funds, GBP 35 million was earmarked for individual compensation to approximately 15,600 Ogoni (approximately GBP 2,200 per claimant), with the rest to benefit the entire community.[5]

The ramifications of Saro-Wiwa's death and the various lawsuits born from his agitation reach far beyond the immediate issues of legal cases and precedents. Saro-Wiwa's story brought corporate accountability and governance to the forefront of the global debate on human rights and the workings of a just society. The effect was so transformative that even academics who side with corporations in their analyses had to adjust their arguments to take Saro-Wiwa into account. In one work, Uwem Ite, who left Lancaster University to join Shell Nigeria, and his protégé, Uwafiokun Idemudia, now at York University in Toronto, claim that the issues facing the Niger Delta require a more nuanced approach but in their analysis claim that corporate entities have little to no power to influence government policies and are unfairly targeted by protest groups. In particular, they claim that "sustainable development in the Niger Delta would require innovative constitutional and institutional reforms, and some kind of 'reinvention of the wheel' of governance in Nigeria."[6] Thus, for Idemudia and Ite, corporations cannot work without the support of the state. While this is plausible reasoning, their analysis assumes that the political roadblocks to sustainable development were in no way the result of collusion between the Nigerian state and the multinational corporations in the first place, and they minimize the strife caused by that collusion. Idemudia goes even further in a subsequent piece and argues that corporations are victims at the hands of the Nigerian government, and though they may wish to implement more socially responsible corporate policies, it is the government's failure to create an environment where these policies are possible that is the main hindrance to corporate development in the Niger Delta.[7]

International corporations have increased their community development work in the Niger Delta, largely due to the negative publicity they received because of Saro-Wiwa. Although some, like Idemudia and Ite, blame the failure of corporate social responsibility (CSR) mainly on the lack of cooperation from the state and the local communities, others investigate whether the companies' CSR policies are solely public relations exercises or genuine attempts to develop cooperative relationships with the communities whose resources they exploit. Many conclude that, when corporate interests and moral imperatives collide, the corporations usually follow the profit motive rather than principles of ethical responsibility. Despite the fact that evidence of the failures of corporate governance in Nigeria emerged largely as a result of Saro-Wiwa's agitation, most of the authors who review the story from a corporate perspective ignore the substantiated allegations that Shell and other companies were not passive observers but actively colluded with the Nigerian military dictatorships to the extent that any future cooperation with local communities would be met with hostility and suspicion.

Ken Saro-Wiwa's legacy has a continuing impact on global discourse in literature, politics, human rights, and the role of corporations in global society. His influence will undoubtedly continue to reverberate in Nigeria and beyond for years to come, and inspire future generations of writers and activists.

# Notes

### Chapter 1: Nigeria and Saro-Wiwa's World to 1960

1. Spelling note: The accepted spelling is Igbo. Historically, other spellings had been used, most notably Ibo. We use the accepted form, except in direct quotations where we maintain the spelling in the original source. Similarly, we use the spelling of Ijo, but keep the still widely accepted Ijaw where it is used in quotations.

2. For clarity, to differentiate the people from the land, we use Ogoniland to denote the land, and Ogoni for the people.

3. This last point would prove especially important when the Abacha regime used the tensions within the Ogoni leadership to execute Saro-Wiwa and the rest of the Ogoni Nine for the murder of four chiefs who rejected MOSOP leadership.

4. Henry Willink et al., "Report of the Commission Appointed to Enquire into the Fears of Minorities and the Means of Allaying Them," ed. Colonial Office (London: Her Majesty's Stationery Office, 1958), 88.

5. Ken Saro-Wiwa, *On a Darkling Plain: An Account of the Nigerian Civil War* (Port Harcourt: Saros, 1989), 88.

6. Richard L. Sklar, *Nigerian Political Parties: Power in an Emergent African Nation* (Princeton: Princeton University Press, 1963), 36.

7. Saro-Wiwa, *On a Darkling Plain*, 24.

### Chapter 2: Saro-Wiwa's Childhood and Education

1. Sonpie Kpone-Tonwe, "Leadership Training in Precolonial Nigeria: The Yaa Tradition of Ogoni," *International Journal of African Historical Studies* 34, no. 2 (2001): 385–86.

2. J. F. Ade Ajayi, "The Development of Secondary Grammar School Education in Nigeria," *Journal of the Historical Society of Nigeria* 2, no. 4 (1963): 521.

3. Amayanabo O. Daminabo, *Ken Saro-Wiwa, 1941–1995: His Life & Legacies* (Buguma, Nigeria: Hanging Gardens Publishers, 2005), 32.

## Chapter 3: The Nigerian Civil War Years

1. Though the coup conspirators are popularly known as the "Five Majors," they counted more than five conspirators and not all of them were majors. However, for clarity's sake, when referring to the coup leaders, I use the popular term "Majors."

2. Ken Saro-Wiwa, *On a Darkling Plain: An Account of the Nigerian Civil War* (Port Harcourt: Saros, 1989), 17.

3. Ibid.

4. Ibid.

5. Ibid., 36.

6. Ibid., 33. Douglas A. Anthony, *Poison and Medicine: Ethnicity, Power, and Violence in a Nigerian City, 1966 to 1986* (Portsmouth, NH: Heinemann; Oxford, UK: James Curry; Cape Town, South Africa: David Philip, 2002), chaps. 2–3.

7. Though the Igbo originated in eastern Nigeria, they had, for generations, lived all over Nigeria. Ojukwu and Azikiwe were both born in Zungeru, in northwestern Nigeria. Nzeogwu's name contains Kaduna, a reference to his place of birth in northern Nigeria. Saro-Wiwa called Nzeogwu the most detribalized of all Nigerians.

8. Saro-Wiwa, *On a Darkling Plain*, 40.

9. Ibid., 10.

10. Ibid., 165.

11. Ken Saro-Wiwa, *A Month and a Day; & Letters*, with a foreword by Wole Soyinka (Banbury, UK: Ayebia, 1995), 50.

## Chapter 4: Business, Writing, and Politics

1. Onukaba Adinoyi Ojo, *Olusegun Obasanjo: In the Eyes of Time* (New York and Lagos: Africana Legacy Press, 1997), 195.

2. Ken Wiwa, *In the Shadow of a Saint : A Son's Journey to Understand His Father's Legacy* (South Royalton, VT: Steerforth Press, 2001), 42–43.

3. Ken Saro-Wiwa, *A Month and a Day; & Letters*, with a foreword by Wole Soyinka (Banbury, UK: Ayebia, 1995), 156.

4. Ken Saro-Wiwa, *Prisoners of Jebs* (Port Harcourt: Saros International, 1988).

5. David Eka, "Aspects of Language in Ken Saro-Wiwa's *Sozaboy: A Novel in Rotten English*," in *Before I Am Hanged: Ken Saro-Wiwa:*

*Literature, Politics and Dissent,* ed. Onookome Okome (Trenton, NJ: Africa World Press, 2000), 75.

6. Chijioke Uwasomba, "War, Violence and Language in Ken Saro-Wiwa's Sozaboy," *Neohelicon* 38, no. 2 (2011): 497.

7. Mary Harvan, "'Its Eventual Victory Is Not in Doubt': An Introduction to the Literature of Ken Saro-Wiwa," *Alif: Journal of Comparative Poetics,* no. 17 (1997): 169.

8. Grace Eche Okereke, "The Female Narrative and Ken Saro-Wiwa's Discourse on Change in *A Forest of Flowers*," in *Before I Am Hanged: Ken Saro-Wiwa: Literature, Politics and Dissent,* ed. Onookome Okome (Trenton, NJ: Africa World Press, 2000).

9. Uzorma Onungwa, *Basi and Company* (Lagos: Nigerian Television Authority, 1985–90).

10. Ken Saro-Wiwa and Peregrino Brimoh, *Mr. B* (Port Harcourt: Saros International, 1987), 82.

11. James Brooke, "Enugu Journal; 30 Million Nigerians Are Laughing at Themselves," *New York Times,* July 24, 1987.

## Chapter 5: Activism and the Politics of Oil, the Environment, and Genocide

1. A rentier state is a state that derives the bulk of its revenue from foreign sources and not from internal revenue collection. Typically, these states derive their income from allowing exploitation of natural resources. For more complete discussions of the concept of the rentier state, see Hazem Luciani Giacomo Beblawi, *The Rentier State* (London: Croom Helm, 1987), and Douglas A. Yates, *The Rentier State in Africa: Oil Rent Dependency and Neocolonialism in the Republic of Gabon* (Trenton, NJ: Africa World Press, 1996).

2. Phia Steyn, "Oil Exploration in Colonial Nigeria, c. 1903–58," *Journal of Imperial and Commonwealth History* 37, no. 2 (2009): 253–54.

3. Ken Saro-Wiwa, *Genocide in Nigeria: The Ogoni Tragedy* (London: Saros International Publishers, 1992).

4. Land Use Act, International Centre for Nigerian Law, http://www.nigeria-law.org/Land%20Use%20Act.htm.

5. Saro-Wiwa, *Genocide in Nigeria*, 54.

6. Ibid., 74.

7. The purchasing power of GBP 3 million in 1973 equates to approximately GBP 48 million in 2014 funds. Source: "Inflation Calculator," Bank of England, http://www.bankofengland.co.uk/education/Pages/resources/inflationtools/calculator/flash/default.aspx. For a detailed discussion of the *Torrey Canyon* spill, see Paul Burrows, Charles

Rowley, and David Owen, "Torrey Canyon: A Case Study in Accidental Pollution," *Scottish Journal of Political Economy* 21, no. 3 (1974): 237–58.

8. "Niger Delta Human Development Report," ed. Alfred Fawundu (Abuja: United Nations Development Programme, 2006), 76.

9. Elisha Jasper Dung, Leonard S. Bombom, and Tano D. Agusomu, "The Effects of Gas Flaring on Crops in the Niger Delta, Nigeria," *GeoJournal* 73, no. 4 (2008): 297–305. For additional studies on the effects of flaring on human and environmental conditions in the Niger Delta, see V. T. Jike, "Environmental Degradation, Social Disequilibrium, and the Dilemma of Sustainable Development in the Niger-Delta of Nigeria," *Journal of Black Studies* 34, no. 5 (2004): 686–701; C. O. Opukri and Ibaba Samuel Ibaba, "Oil-Induced Environmental Degradation and Internal Population Displacement in Nigeria's Niger Delta," *Journal of Sustainable Development in Africa* 10, no. 1 (2008): 180–85.

10. Marcus Edino, Godwin Nsofor, and Leonard Bombom, "Perceptions and Attitudes towards Gas Flaring in the Niger Delta, Nigeria," *Environmentalist* 30, no. 1 (2010): 74.

11. Jike, "Environmental Degradation, Social Disequilibrium, and the Dilemma of Sustainable Development," 694. For more on the urban migration in Nigeria see Andrew G. Onokerhoraye, "Case Studies of Urban Slums and Environmental Problems in Nigerian Cities," in *Environmental Issues and Management in Nigerian Development,* ed. Pius O. Sada and F. O. Odemerho (Ibadan, Nigeria: Evans Brothers [Nigeria Publishers], 1988); For a broader discussion of the issues facing Niger Delta residents, see Bronwen Manby and Human Rights Watch, *The Price of Oil: Corporate Responsibility and Human Rights Violations in Nigeria's Oil-Producing Communities* (New York: Human Rights Watch, 1999).

12. Saro-Wiwa, *Genocide in Nigeria,* 89–90.

13. Steyn, "Oil Exploration in Colonial Nigeria, c. 1903–58," 262–63.

14. Narasingha P. Sil, "Nigerian Intellectuals and Socialism: Retrospect and Prospect," *Journal of Modern African Studies* 31, no. 3 (1993): 361–85.

15. A short promotional documentary was made by Philip Gaunt, "Festac 77—Lagos Festival" (UNESCO TV, 1977). The film is widely available online.

16. For a brief but in-depth overview of the Maitatsine revolt, see Elizabeth Isichei, "The Maitatsine Risings in Nigeria, 1980–85: A Revolt of the Disinherited," *Journal of Religion in Africa* 17, no. 3 (1987): 194–208.

17. Isaac Jasper Adaka Boro and Anthony Odogboro Tebekaemi, *The Twelve-Day Revolution* (Benin City: Idodo Umeh Publishers, 1982). Online version available at http://www.adakaboro.org/.

18. Ibid.

19. Ibid.

## Chapter 6: MOSOP, the Ogoni Bill of Rights, and Saro-Wiwa's Activism

1. Ken Saro-Wiwa, *Genocide in Nigeria: The Ogoni Tragedy* (London: Saros International Publishers, 1992), 7.

2. Ken Wiwa, *In the Shadow of a Saint: A Son's Journey to Understand His Father's Legacy* (South Royalton, VT: Steerforth Press, 2001), 48. National Electric Power Authority is the correct name abbreviated as NEPA.

3. Saro-Wiwa, *Genocide in Nigeria*, 94.

4. Ibid., 95.

5. Ken Saro-Wiwa, *A Month and a Day; & Letters*, with a foreword by Wole Soyinka (Banbury, UK: Ayebia, 1995), 54.

6. Ibid., 61.

7. Ibid., 55.

8. Ibid., 100.

9. Raphael Lemkin and Carnegie Endowment for International Peace Division of International Law, *Axis Rule in Occupied Europe: Laws of Occupation, Analysis of Government, Proposals for Redress* (Washington, DC: Carnegie Endowment for International Peace, Division of International Law, 1944).

10. "Convention on the Prevention and Punishment of the Crime of Genocide," United Nations Treaty Collection, https://treaties.un.org/doc/Publication/UNTS/Volume%2078/volume-78-I-1021-English.pdf.

11. Saro-Wiwa, *Genocide in Nigeria*, 99.

12. Ibid., 81.

13. Ibid., 83.

14. Ibid., 91.

15. Ibid.

16. A full account of the affair can be found in Gordon Thomas, *Gideon's Spies: The Secret History of the Mossad* (New York: St. Martin's Press, 1999), chap. 13.

17. For a description of the "environmental," the colloquial name for a popular cleanup program, see Denis C. E. Ugwuegbu, *Social Psychology and Social Change in Nigeria : A Systematic Evaluation of Government Social Policies and Programs* (Bloomington, IN:

IUniverse Inc., 2011), 300–303. A depiction of the communal spirit of the "environmental" is visible in Gavin Searle and David Harewood, *Welcome to Lagos* (London: BBC, 2010).

18. In other parts of the world, the bags have similar xenophobic names. In Germany, they have been referred to as *Tuekenkoffer,* or Turkish suitcase. In the United Kingdom they were called Bangladeshi bags, because of the influx of refugees fleeing to Britain with similar bags to escape the 1971 Bangladesh war. In 2007, fashion designer Louis Vuitton created a bag line based on the design with the firm's iconic logo. Dolly Jones, "Spring/Summer 2007 | Ready to Wear: Louis Vuitton," *Vogue,* http://www.vogue.co.uk/fashion/spring -summer-2007/ready-to-wear/louis-vuitton.

19. J. Timothy Hunt, *The Politics of Bones: Dr. Owens Wiwa and the Struggle for Nigeria's Oil* (Toronto: M&S, 2005), 58.

20. Saro-Wiwa, *A Month and a Day; & Letters,* 72.

21. Ibid., 91.

22. "Shell Paid Nigerian Army," *Earth Island Journal* 12, no. 2 (1997): 16.

23. Kenneth B. Noble, "Nigerian Military Rulers Annul Election," *New York Times,* June 24, 1993.

24. Saro-Wiwa, *A Month and a Day; & Letters,* 171.


## Chapter 7: The Trials and Death of Saro-Wiwa

1. Transparency International, *Global Corruption Report 2004* (London: Pluto Press, 2004), 13.

2. Karl Maier, *This House Has Fallen: Midnight in Nigeria* (New York: PublicAffairs, 2000), 101.

3. Melissa Crow, "Nigeria: The Ogoni Crisis: A Case Study of Military Repression in Southeastern Nigeria" (New York: Human Rights Watch/Africa, 1995). Online version available at http://www .hrw.org/reports/1995/Nigeria.htm.

4. Andy Rowell, "Oil, Shell, and Nigeria: Ken Saro-Wiwa Calls for a Boycott," *Ecologist* 25 (1995): 212.

5. Andy Rowell and Eveline Lubbers, "Ken Saro-Wiwa Was Framed, Secret Evidence Shows," *Independent on Sunday,* December 5, 2010.

6. Amayanabo O. Daminabo, *Ken Saro-Wiwa, 1941–1995: His Life & Legacies* (Buguma, Nigeria: Hanging Gardens Publishers, 2005), 293.

7. The initial report appeared in Rowell and Lubbers, "Ken Saro-Wiwa Was Framed, Secret Evidence Shows." Rowell later released a fuller account through the organization Oil Change International,

which can be found at Andy Rowell, "Saro-Wiwa Was Framed, New Evidence Shows," Oil Change International, http://priceofoil .org/2010/12/06/saro-wiwa-was-framed-new-evidence-shows/. The accounts are taken from Ejiogu's testimony, which was to be submitted as evidence in the case of *Wiwa v. Royal Dutch Shell Co.*, which was settled out of court days before the trial was set to begin. Discussion of the trial appears in the next chapter.

8. Crow, "Nigeria: The Ogoni Crisis."

9. Ibid.

10. Ibid.

11. Ibid.

12. Ibid.

13. Ibid.

14. Oronto N. Douglas, "Ogoni: Four Days of Brutality and Torture," *Liberty,* May–August 1994, 21–22.

15. Ibid.

16. Michael Birnbaum, "Nigeria Fundamental Rights Denied: Report of the Trial of Ken Saro-Wiwa and Others" (London: Article 19, the International Centre Against Censorship, 1995). Appendix 5A.

17. Ibid., 47–48.

18. Maier, *This House Has Fallen,* 108.

19. Michael Birnbaum, "Judicial Travesty Preordained the Final Verdict: Execution of Ken Saro-Wiwa: Legal View," *Times,* November 13, 1995.

20. Birnbaum, "Nigeria Fundamental Rights Denied," 43.

21. Crow, "Nigeria: The Ogoni Crisis."

22. Sonia Shah, *Crude: The Story of Oil* (New York: Seven Stories Press, 2004), 98.

23. Birnbaum, "Judicial Travesty Preordained the Final Verdict."

24. Ibid.

25. Ken Saro-Wiwa, *A Month and a Day; & Letters,* with a foreword by Wole Soyinka (Banbury, UK: Ayebia, 1995).

26. Daminabo, *Ken Saro-Wiwa,* 339–40; Frank Aigbogun, Associated Press Lagos, "It Took Five Tries to Hang Saro-Wiwa," *Independent,* November 13, 1995.

27. Ken Wiwa, *In the Shadow of a Saint: A Son's Journey to Understand His Father's Legacy* (South Royalton, VT: Steerforth Press, 2001), 161.

28. Clifford Bob, *The Marketing of Rebellion: Insurgents, Media, and International Activism* (Cambridge: Cambridge University Press, 2005), 101–4.

## Chapter 8: The Many Legacies of Ken Saro-Wiwa

1. Allan Gregg, "Allan Gregg in Conversation with Ken Wiwa" (Toronto: TVOntario, 2003).

2. Kehinde A. Ayoola, "*Things Fall Apart* as the *Avant-Courier* of the Nigerian Variety of English," in *Blazing the Path: Fifty Years of Things Fall Apart,* ed. Chima Anyadike and Kehinde A. Ayoola (Ibadan: HEBN Publishers, 2012), 195.

3. Ken Wiwa, *In the Shadow of a Saint: A Son's Journey to Understand His Father's Legacy* (South Royalton, VT: Steerforth Press, 2001), i.

4. Noo Saro-Wiwa, *Looking for Transwonderland: Travels in Nigeria* (Berkeley, CA: Soft Skull Press, 2012), 229–31. Motorcycle taxis in Nigeria are popularly called okadas because one of the first airlines in Nigeria, Okada Air, advertised itself as a quick way to travel in Nigeria. Similarly, the motorcycle taxis can travel quickly through Nigeria's traffic and have proven a speedy, if uncomfortable, way to travel in Nigeria's urban centers. Okadas are banned in Nigeria's capital, Abuja, and have been facing severe restrictions in recent years, such as in Lagos where since 2012 they have been restricted to certain roadways.

5. Elisha Bala-Gbogbo, "Shell to Pay $83 Million Settlement for Nigeria Oil Spills," *Bloomberg Business,* January 7, 2015. Online at http://www.bloomberg.com/news/articles/2015-01-07/shell-agrees -83-million-settlement-for-nigeria-bodo-oil-spills (accessed December 3, 2015).

6. Uwafiokun Idemudia and Uwem E. Ite, "Demystifying the Niger Delta Conflict: Towards an Integrated Explanation," *Review of African Political Economy* 33, no. 109 (2006): 403.

7. Uwafiokun Idemudia, "Corporate Social Responsibility and the Rentier Nigerian State: Rethinking the Role of Government and the Possibility of Corporate Social Development in the Niger Delta," *Canadian Journal of Development Studies / Revue canadienne d'études du développement* 30, no. 1–2 (2010): 131–51.

# Bibliography

Ajayi, J. F. Ade. "The Development of Secondary Grammar School Education in Nigeria." *Journal of the Historical Society of Nigeria* 2, no. 4 (1963): 517–35.

Anthony, Douglas A. *Poison and Medicine: Ethnicity, Power, and Violence in a Nigerian City, 1966 to 1986.* Portsmouth, NH: Heinemann; Oxford, UK: James Currey; Cape Town, South Africa: David Philip, 2002.

Ayoola, Kehinde A. "Things Fall Apart as the Avant-Courier of the Nigerian Variety of English." In *Blazing the Path: Fifty Years of Things Fall Apart,* edited by Chima Anyadike and Kehinde A. Ayoola. Ibadan: HEBN Publishers, 2012.

Beblawi, Hazem Luciani Giacomo. *The Rentier State.* London: Croom Helm, 1987.

Birnbaum, Michael. "Nigeria Fundamental Rights Denied: Report of the Trial of Ken Saro-Wiwa and Others." London: Article 19, the International Centre Against Censorship, 1995.

Bob, Clifford. *The Marketing of Rebellion: Insurgents, Media, and International Activism.* Cambridge: Cambridge University Press, 2005.

Boro, Isaac Jasper Adaka, and Anthony Odogboro Tebekaemi. *The Twelve-Day Revolution.* Benin City: Idodo Umeh Publishers, 1982.

Burrows, Paul, Charles Rowley, and David Owen. "Torrey Canyon: A Case Study in Accidental Pollution." *Scottish Journal of Political Economy* 21, no. 3 (1974): 237–58.

"Convention on the Prevention and Punishment of the Crime of Genocide." United Nations Treaty Collection, https://treaties.un.org/doc/Publication/UNTS/Volume%2078/volume-78-I-1021-English.pdf.

Crow, Melissa, and Human Rights Watch/Africa. "Nigeria: The Ogoni Crisis: A Case Study of Military Repression in Southeastern Nigeria." New York: Human Rights Watch/Africa, 1995.

Daminabo, Amayanabo O. *Ken Saro-Wiwa, 1941–1995: His Life & Legacies.* Buguma, Nigeria: Hanging Gardens Publishers, 2005.

Douglas, Oronto N. "Ogoni: Four Days of Brutality and Torture." *Liberty,* May–August 1994, 21–22.

Dung, Elisha Jasper, Leonard S. Bombom, and Tano D. Agusomu. "The Effects of Gas Flaring on Crops in the Niger Delta, Nigeria." *GeoJournal* 73, no. 4 (2008): 297–305.

Eche Okereke, Grace. "The Female Narrative and Ken Saro-Wiwa's Discourse on Change in *A Forest of Flowers.*" In *Before I Am Hanged: Ken Saro-Wiwa: Literature, Politics and Dissent,* edited by Onookome Okome, 123–36. Trenton, NJ: Africa World Press, 2000.

Edino, Marcus, Godwin Nsofor, and Leonard Bombom. "Perceptions and Attitudes towards Gas Flaring in the Niger Delta, Nigeria." *Environmentalist* 30, no. 1 (2010): 67–75.

Eka, David. "Aspects of Language in Ken Saro-Wiwa's *Sozaboy: A Novel in Rotten English.*" In *Before I Am Hanged: Ken Saro-Wiwa: Literature, Politics and Dissent,* edited by Onookome Okome. Trenton, NJ: Africa World Press, 2000.

Gaunt, Philip, director. "Festac 77—Lagos Festival." 26 minutes. UNESCO TV, 1977.

Gregg, Allan. "Allan Gregg in Conversation with Ken Wiwa." 25 minutes. Toronto: TVOntario, 2003.

Harvan, Mary. "'Its Eventual Victory Is Not in Doubt': An Introduction to the Literature of Ken Saro-Wiwa." *Alif: Journal of Comparative Poetics,* no. 17 (1997): 161–82.

Hunt, J. Timothy. *The Politics of Bones: Dr. Owens Wiwa and the Struggle for Nigeria's Oil.* Toronto: M&S, 2005.

Idemudia, Uwafiokun. "Corporate Social Responsibility and the Rentier Nigerian State: Rethinking the Role of Government and the Possibility of Corporate Social Development in the Niger Delta." *Canadian Journal of Development Studies / Revue canadienne d'études du développement* 30, no. 1–2 (2010): 131–51.

Idemudia, Uwafiokun, and Uwem E. Ite. "Demystifying the Niger Delta Conflict: Towards an Integrated Explanation." *Review of African Political Economy* 33, no. 109 (2006): 391–406.

"Inflation Calculator." Bank of England, http://www.bankofengland .co.uk/education/Pages/resources/inflationtools/calculator /flash/default.aspx.

Isichei, Elizabeth. "The Maitatsine Risings in Nigeria, 1980–85: A Revolt of the Disinherited." *Journal of Religion in Africa* 17, no. 3 (1987): 194–208.

Jike, V. T. "Environmental Degradation, Social Disequilibrium, and the Dilemma of Sustainable Development in the Niger-Delta of Nigeria." *Journal of Black Studies* 34, no. 5 (2004): 686–701.

Jones, Dolly. "Spring/Summer 2007 | Ready to Wear: Louis Vuitton." *Vogue,* http://www.vogue.co.uk/fashion/spring-summer-2007 /ready-to-wear/louis-vuitton.

Kpone-Tonwe, Sonpie. "Leadership Training in Precolonial Nigeria: The Yaa Tradition of Ogoni." *International Journal of African Historical Studies* 34, no. 2 (2001): 385–86.

"Land Use Act." International Centre for Nigerian Law, http://www .nigeria-law.org/Land%20Use%20Act.htm.

Lemkin, Raphael, and Carnegie Endowment for International Peace Division of International Law. *Axis Rule in Occupied Europe: Laws of Occupation, Analysis of Government, Proposals for Redress.* Washington, DC: Carnegie Endowment for International Peace, Division of International Law, 1944.

Maier, Karl. *This House Has Fallen: Midnight in Nigeria.* New York: PublicAffairs, 2000.

Manby, Bronwen, and Human Rights Watch. *The Price of Oil: Corporate Responsibility and Human Rights Violations in Nigeria's Oil-Producing Communities.* New York: Human Rights Watch, 1999.

"Niger Delta Human Development Report." Edited by Alfred Fawundu. Abuja: United Nations Development Programme, 2006.

Ojo, Onukaba Adinoyi. *Olusegun Obasanjo: In the Eyes of Time.* New York and Lagos: Africana Legacy Press, 1997.

Okome, Onookome, ed. *Before I Am Hanged: Ken Saro-Wiwa: Literature, Politics and Dissent.* Trenton, NJ: Africa World Press, 2000.

Onokerhoraye, Andrew G. "Case Studies of Urban Slums and Environmental Problems in Nigerian Cities." In *Environmental Issues and Management in Nigerian Development,* edited by Pius O. Sada and F. O. Odemerho. Ibadan, Nigeria: Evans Brothers (Nigeria Publishers), 1988.

Onungwa, Uzorma, director. *Basi and Company.* Lagos, Nigeria: Nigerian Television Authority, 1985–1990.

Opukri, C. O., and Ibaba Samuel Ibaba. "Oil-Induced Environmental Degradation and Internal Population Displacement in Nigeria's Niger Delta." *Journal of Sustainable Development in Africa* 10, no. 1 (2008). Online at http://www.jsd-africa.com/Jsda/V10N1 _Spring2008/PDF/OilInducedEnvDegr.pdf.

Rowell, Andy. "Oil, Shell and Nigeria: Ken Saro-Wiwa Calls for a Boycott." *Ecologist* 25 (November–December 1995): 210+.

———. "Saro-Wiwa Was Framed, New Evidence Shows." Oil Change International, http://priceofoil.org/2010/12/06/saro-wiwa-was-framed-new-evidence-shows/.

Rowell, Andy, and Eveline Lubbers. "Ken Saro-Wiwa Was Framed, Secret Evidence Shows." *Independent on Sunday*, December 5, 2010.

Saro-Wiwa, Ken. *Genocide in Nigeria: The Ogoni Tragedy* [in English]. London: Saros International Publishers, 1992.

———. *A Month and a Day; & Letters.* Foreword by Wole Soyinka. Banbury, UK: Ayebia, 1995.

———. *On a Darkling Plain: An Account of the Nigerian Civil War.* Port Harcourt: Saros, 1989.

———. *Prisoners of Jebs* [in English]. Saros International, 1988.

Saro-Wiwa, Ken, and Peregrino Brimoh. *Mr. B.* Port Harcourt: Saros International, 1987.

Saro-Wiwa, Noo. *Looking for Transwonderland: Travels in Nigeria* [in English]. Berkeley, CA: Soft Skull Press, 2012.

Searle, Gavin, and David Harewood. *Welcome to Lagos.* London: BBC, 2010.

Shah, Sonia. *Crude: The Story of Oil* [in English]. New York: Seven Stories Press, 2004.

"Shell Paid Nigerian Army." *Earth Island Journal* 12, no. 2 (Spring 1997): 16.

Sil, Narasingha P. "Nigerian Intellectuals and Socialism: Retrospect and Prospect." *Journal of Modern African Studies* 31, no. 3 (1993): 361–85.

Sklar, Richard L. *Nigerian Political Parties: Power in an Emergent African Nation.* Princeton: Princeton University Press, 1963.

Steyn, Phia. "Oil Exploration in Colonial Nigeria, c. 1903–58." *Journal of Imperial and Commonwealth History* 37, no. 2 (2009): 249–74.

Thomas, Gordon. *Gideon's Spies: The Secret History of the Mossad* [in English]. New York: St. Martin's Press, 1999.

Transparency International. *Global Corruption Report 2004.* London: Pluto Press, 2004.

Ugwuegbu, Denis C. E. *Social Psychology and Social Change in Nigeria: A Systematic Evaluation of Government Social Policies and Programs* [in English]. Bloomington, IN: IUniverse Inc., 2011.

Uwasomba, Chijioke. "War, Violence and Language in Ken Saro-Wiwa's Sozaboy" [in English]. *Neohelicon* 38, no. 2 (December 2011): 487–98.

Willink, Henry, et al. "Report of the Commission Appointed to Enquire into the Fears of Minorities and the Means of Allaying

Them." Edited by the Colonial Office. London: Her Majesty's Stationery Office, 1958.

Wiwa, Ken. *In the Shadow of a Saint: A Son's Journey to Understand His Father's Legacy* [in English]. South Royalton, VT: Steerforth Press, 2001.

Yates, Douglas A. *The Rentier State in Africa: Oil Rent Dependency and Neocolonialism in the Republic of Gabon* [in English]. Trenton, NJ: Africa World Press, 1996.

# Index